Praise for Dark-Land

"In *Dark-Land*, Kevin Hart has crafted a personal narrative of searing beauty, a portrait of an extinct place and time and one boy's roiling development within it. This is not only a poet's Proustian grasping after memory, but a melodic assertion of selfhood and how that selfhood is forged within the contradictions of family and the pronouncements of faith. Put this beautiful book on your shelf between Frank Conroy's *Stop-Time* and Tobias Wolff's *This Boy's Life*."
—William Giraldi, author of *The Hero's Body*

"This is a profoundly meditative book, philosophical in its sweep and magnificent in its phrasing, which encompasses rape and religion, Jewishness and Catholicism, and the darkness of those places where we grope for what truth the self may fumble towards."
—Peter Craven, *Australian cultural critic*

"The memories that make their way into words here, emerging with startling clarity from the fog of forgetting, trace a highly unusual life journey from childhood into adolescence and beyond, and from working-class post-War London to steamy Brisbane in the sizzling '60s and ultimately to the USA. More than a memoir, Hart's *Dark-Land* is also a sustained meditation on the enduring mysteries of mind and a compelling evocation of particular social milieux during a time of escalating if patchy geohistorical change. Lyrical, brooding, and at times hilariously funny, this is an utterly riveting read."
—Kate Rigby, Alexander von Humboldt Professor of Environmental Humanities, University of Cologne, author of *Meditations on Creation in an Era of Extinction*

"Luminously detailed and lovingly told, *Dark-Land* is a memoir I will not soon forget. From the 'divided life' of his working-class childhood in London's East End to his family's immigration to sweltering Queensland, Kevin Hart tells of a boy who sees everything through a fog of unknowing, until a series of epiphanies opens the world to him. A major philosopher and theologian, Hart is also one of the finest poets now at work in English. In this remarkable coming-of-age, he writes, 'Childhood ends, and then it ends again, and then it ends yet again.' But as the story proves, it never does."

—David Mason, author of *Incarnation and Metamorphosis: Can Literature Change Us?*

DARK-LAND

DARK-LAND

Memoir of a Secret Childhood

Kevin Hart

pdb

PAUL DRY BOOKS
Philadelphia 2024

First Paul Dry Books Edition, 2024

Paul Dry Books, Inc.
Philadelphia, Pennsylvania
www.pauldrybooks.com

Copyright © 2024 Kevin Hart

All rights reserved.

Printed in the United States of America

Library of Congress Control Number: 2024932345

ISBN: 978-1-58988-189-1.

In memory:

James Oliver Wotton (1903-80)
Rosina Mary Wotton (1900-82)
James Henry Hart (1918-2009)
Rosina Mary Hart (1924-87)
Pauline Wolstenholme (1945-2020)

It must have tears
And memory and claws

—Wallace Stevens

Contents

Acknowledgments

I would like to thank Ms. Merryl Macey for supplying me with material about Goodna State School in the period I was studying there, and Mr. Rodney Iffinger for doing the same with regard to Corinda State School. Peter van Twist and Bryan Wharton kindly jogged my memory about several events in my early teens. I am indebted to several friends who read one or another draft of this memoir and made comments on aspects of it that have helped me to complete the work: Alexandra Aidler, Larry Bouchard, Gavin Flood, Phil Gates, Charlie Gillespie, Paul Kane, Kate Rigby, David Mason, Beth Frazier, and David Tracy. In particular, Dan O'Neill made many useful suggestions—his eagle eye and faultless ear have improved the book beyond measure—and my wife, Sashanna Hart, read the whole, made apt suggestions, and her affirmation of it has made the whole undertaking worthwhile for me. Finally, my thanks to the editorial and production team at Paul Dry Books for their exemplary work in bringing the book into the world.

1 ▸

Sometimes I was woken up by the sound: icy bottles of milk being clumped down on the doorstep round about five of a winter's morning. By the time I got out of bed they had been set before the paraffin heater in the living room, but the thick cream of the fresh milk was still cold on the tongue. I eased off the crimped foil top, good for flicking around when playing with Bobbie the cat, and scooped out the top of the milk with a finger still warm from sleep. I left the sterilized milk alone; it tasted vile.

It was easy to freeze when no longer under the heap of blankets. My shirt and trousers were usually stiff before I clambered into them. The school was two doors down; the bell announced tight quick rabbit punches in the corridor, incomprehensible lessons, boredom, and teachers with long, ribbed canes. Yet it was good to be there early, especially in the great fogs, the peasoupers. Breakfast was a slice of toast with a scraping of marge that I could take right out the door. We would play hide and seek in the playground by just standing still: I would hold out my arm and not see my hand. Invisible even to myself, I would breathe in the dense sooty cloud, longing for the bell not to ring. Someone would bang into me, or I'd see a shape looming before me and quietly step back into occult gray to escape again. And then the bell: blunt, brassy clangs. Light glowered from a big door opening, and we slouched in.

In the classroom I always wanted to have a seat near the wall, next to one of those radiators thumping out dusty heat, but there was no year I was not put right in the middle of the classroom; I was brought up cold. Not good at anything, the only job I could do was filling inkwells. The bottle was large, squat; its blue-black ink poured out in a great rush if you didn't watch out. On some days leftover ink had frozen overnight, and I had to break it up with an old wooden pen with a clogged metal nib before pouring in some more. But now the radiators were on; in a while it would be warm near the walls; it was an easy job and a dry one, and one I could do alone. I made it last: if things went well, if there was enough ice to crack and no one was around, I managed to string it out and be late for morning hymns. Sometimes I would listen to a couple of them from the classroom. Strains of "All fings bright and beau'iful" would seep under the closed door, though no one singing it had ever seen a "purple-headed mountain" or dawdled in a meadow with rushes nearby. More often, "Mornin' 'as bro-ken" would fill the classroom while I worked. How could the singing of where Jesus's feet passed mean anything to me or to any of the kids I knew? I had little or no idea who Jesus was, and I doubt that they did, either. Yet I loved the line about "the sweetness of the wet garden." I knew the look of hollyhocks with raindrops and daffodils with their big heads nodding in the rain. I also thrilled a little at the conjunction of *sweet* and *wet*, though I had no idea why and no interest in finding out. The question slumbered in my mind.

One of the older female teachers would roam around the gym during hymns and listen as you sang. There was a singing competition in Barking once a year, at which the school had not done well, and the Headmaster wanted Thomas Arnold to improve on its poor ranking in 1962. If the teacher touched you on the shoulder, you sat down. It meant that you were out of tune and had to be quiet. I was always touched if I was there, even during "He Who Would True Valour See" and "Jerusalem," which surged through me in huge, uncontrollable waves breaking from the piano, bringing forth stretched notes, wildly flat or wildly sharp. I did not know at the time that the lyrics of the latter hymn were by William Blake, I only thought how peculiar it was that we were singing with gusto again about the feet of this man, Jesus, who must have trudged around England a long time ago, apparently without socks and shoes. He must have been cold, too. So I cracked black ice and poured the ink slowly, standing by the radiators every now and then, not in any hurry to get to hymns. When I would finally reach the hall the music spilled out in a rush on opening the door, and I would go quietly to the back. Walking in, there was one of those old women banging away at the piano, looking over her shoulder at the assembled kids. "You see," she would say looking over her glasses, "I'm clever. I can play *and* see what you're up to." But she never saw me leaning by the radiator in the classroom down the hall, waiting for time to pass. And she hadn't seen us boys punishing anyone who coughed too loud and was found when playing hide and seek, pushing his finger onto a frozen pipe so that he would lose a layer of skin to it when he pulled away.

Every so often one of the teachers would address the school after hymns. Once there was a very old man, Mr. Silver, who had white hair, wore a dark suit, and who spoke about his memories of the war, of his son being killed, and we all got restless. "If you don't want to hear me, I'll just stop," he said, clearly wounded. Male teachers, stationed around the gym, started swishing their canes near their thickly trousered legs. I could see that the tip of Fergie's cane was frayed. Then one of the big uns sent a whisper round, "Keep quiet, or we'll 'ave to go to class an' bloody *work*!" We all knew he was right, so we sat still in the gym, legs crossed, mostly listening to kids fart, one following the other along the row, until the old man dried up completely and we were all led off down the corridor.

—— ▼ ——

We never saw Mr. Silver again, and he was never mentioned by any of the teachers. One Monday morning I shuffled into hymns about halfway through, but there was no singing. The Headmaster, Mr. Benfield, was talking tightly and fiercely. Some money had been stolen from the office on the weekend. "I want whoever has done this to own up," he said in a commanding voice. There was a vast pause. "I'll give that boy a thrashing he won't forget," he said. (Another pause with a bruising look.) "And then he'll go home and get another thrashing from his father." He held us firmly with his eye, his pepper and salt moustache not even trembling above his lip, and then eventually stepped sharply off the stage. For a day or two the entire school crouched before the reptilian eyes of teachers, and then no more was heard of it. We played in the smog. It seems that Benfield's attractive proposal had not enticed anyone to come forward.

Then Benfield ruled that half of the playground was out of bounds. Only the big kids, those in the top form, could be in one part of it, and the rest of us had to stay in the other part. So there was no football between "us an' 'em," as we had relished, no hide and seek in the fog with the big kids, and doing anything with them gave it an edge. It was a silent, blanket punishment for the theft. So we kicked a soccer ball around in our part of the playground, sometimes being hit full in the face with a fast wet ball because you couldn't see it coming. Once it went straight past me, and I followed it. A teacher was standing there in the fog, "Fergie": Welsh, red-faced, with a deep brown voice, he was known for his strictness and theatrical displays of temper. He grabbed my arm, and, missing his aim, slammed down his thick cane on my wrist with a sudden whistle for being "out of bounds." I didn't tell my parents about the welt on my wrist. It was winter, after all. I pulled my jumper down an extra inch and went to bed as early as I could.

—— ▼ ——

There was always bullying at school, but in my penultimate year at Thomas Arnold it became intense. It usually took the form of being picked on by bigger boys or boys from the rougher families. "'ere, were yer lookin' at me, sunshine?" And then would come a punch in the stomach. "Better get me some crisps from the Tuck Shop, there's more where that came from!" Or I would be taunted. "Jam tart! Jam tart!" I would get day after day. I'd put up with it for a long while, anger slowly building up, until one day the cyst suddenly burst. One boy had been needling me for days, threatening to get me after school, and trying to pinch my Tuck Shop money from my desk. Towards the end of lunchtime, he started with his litany of taunts. I simply ran towards him, leapt higher than I ever thought I could, and landed smack bang on top of him. He fell to the ground with me right on him, and bashed his head on the concrete, right next to a faded square of a hopscotch game. I didn't need to punch him; when he got up he was dazed and looked at me strangely. A bunch of big uns had knotted round; they too looked at me in a new way. Everyone dispersed before a teacher could find us, and I went off with my mates. I was never bullied again in that school.

That same year I had a female teacher who kept telling us all to be *sensible*, as though the word tasted of a sour lemon she was obliged to have in her mouth purely by virtue of having been born British. Once, in a test, one of her questions read, "How many hours are there in a day?" I thought this must be a trick, since a day consists of a day and a night, and since nights in winter were about as long as days, I reasoned, I gave my answer as twelve. Naturally enough, the answer was marked incorrect. Perplexed, I went to the teacher's desk and pointed out that my answer had been marked wrong when it was right. "It's *not* right," she said, as if putting down a brick. "If there are twenty-four hours in a day, where does the night go?" I asked. "It's part of the day," she said, somewhat surprised. "But we 'ave days and we 'ave nights," I countered, sure of my ground. "Just be *sensible*," she sighed, and pointed me back to my seat. "Dunno who sleeps in the day, unless it's Dad," I muttered to myself as I walked back to my seat.

Girls in our class who were convicted of not being sensible, which turned out to be all too often, were told to present themselves to her desk. (Boys were sent to Fergie or Benfield for the same lapses in British civility.) The first time I saw this spectacle was at the end of a day at the start of the year. She had called a curly-haired girl from the back of the class who had been talking while she was talking, which was a cardinal sin. The girl was always a bit prim; she rose slowly and walked, head bowed, up to the front of the class, and the teacher told her to put her hands on the side of the desk. She took out a white plimsoll from one of her desk drawers, told the girl to stick out her bottom, and then hit her hard. The girl, though, was wearing a white taffeta dress, highly unusual in that school, and since it flounced as she walked it must have had many layers. So the teacher was not at all satisfied. She dragged her chair from behind her desk, sat down, and pulled the girl's arm roughly so that she fell over her lap, facing us.

Teacher lifted her skirt, and gave her three or four tremendous thwacks with the plimsoll. We had all read *Dennis the Menace*, so we knew about slippering, but this was no cartoon. How could this be happening? The girl hadn't done anything remotely as bad as what Dennis did week after week. I could see her face get redder and redder as she wailed, then screamed, and tears poured down her face in a thunderstorm, as much from embarrassment as from pain, I knew even then. The whole thing lasted only a minute, then the girl waded back in shame to her desk. We were quiet as midnight, some kids looking down at their desks; even the teacher was a bit shaky, but she managed to say, with her lemon now nicely back in place, "Next time the boys'll see

what you got. And don't come to school again in that dress!"
Almost every week it happened to someone or other. If it wasn't
the slipper, it was a ruler on the hand. And tougher boys were
sent out, once or twice a week, to Benfield or Fergie, for talking,
not working, passing notes, farting on purpose, flicking balls of
snot, or worse, with a note saying how many strokes of the cane
were recommended: usually one, two, four, or six. Once Fergie
came into class to cane a boy. He had him stand in front of us
all, and hold out his hand. Down came the cane with a whistle,
but at the last moment the boy pulled back his hand, and Fergie managed to hit himself on the leg. He was livid. The boy was
taken outside where another male teacher gripped his arms, one
after another, and we heard him get six cuts. He came back in
as though he had been filleted. Somehow, though, the slippering
of the girl was worse. At least the boy could stand when it was
happening.

When I got home, all of fifteen minutes after it had happened,
Mum asked, "Wot's 'appened to you? You're white as a ghost!" I
told her. I thought she would be shocked. "That's nothin', boy,"
she said. "When I was a girl, an' 'ad done somethin', Granddad'd
go on the warpath." (Pause.) "'I'll 'ave your guts for garters,
girl!' 'e'd say. Then 'e'd take off 'is leather belt, an' hold me over
the side of the settee, an' lay into me. 'e belted the backs of my
thighs somethin' awful. Just rememberin' the sound of 'im takin'
off that belt makes me feel shaky even now."

The weeks dragged on. Then, one afternoon up in my room, I
decided I would pretend to be sick so as not to have to go back.
I hit upon constipation as my malady, which turned out to be a
good choice. "'ow can the boy go to school, if 'e suddenly has to
go?" asked my mother of my doubtful father; the question proved
to be unanswerable. So I would stay at home, go shopping down
Broad Street with Mum and carry home the cloth she would
buy for her dressmaking business, help her a bit with sewing by

covering buttons, read comics, play with lead soldiers or plastic
dinosaurs, and have some McVitie's Jaffa cakes, custard creams,
or lemon puffs while watching Bill and Ben the Flowerpot Men
on TV and trying to talk to Kim, our poodle, in Oddle Poddle
while he spoke back in Odd Poodle. Days just crept by, turned
down low. Somehow I filled an hour by dancing around and singing to myself in a tuneless sort of way,

> *Here we go Looby Loo*
> *Here we go Looby Light*
> *Here we go Looby Loo*
> *All on a Saturday night!*

Did I pick that up from a repeat of *Andy Pandy* on TV or from
the playground where it had probably been passed on from one
class to another since who knows when? Now and then at lunchtime a girl would be sent from a group of girls milling around by
the fence, several looking sideways at us, to ask if we boys would
join in a game of it, and more often than not we'd kick our ball
into a corner and looby around with them until the bell went.
Once you started the song, there was a storm of hair flying, feet
stamping, and hands slapping; we were absorbed by a game that
had always been going on, with us or without us, one that had no
reason ever to stop.

At any rate, I think my mother liked me being at home for the
company, Dad being out at work or upstairs asleep so much of
the time, and I loved the intimate fragrance of dresses freshly
pressed with a steam iron. Completely implausibly, I managed
to string out having constipation for six long weeks, visiting the
carsey in the middle of the night, by which time the local doctor
said I'd have to have an enema. The thought of a rubber tube
being stuck up my bottom and hot water being run through it
was too much. The next day I told my parents that I had been

sitting on the throne all night and all was fine, so I reluctantly resumed going to school.

———— ▾ ————

While I had been lounging around at home, something new had happened at the school: we were all going to learn how to swim. Most of us had been down to the seaside for holidays and had splashed around in the water, but I don't think that any of us had ever learned to swim. We boys were very excited; we'd miss out on a whole afternoon of school *and* get to see Pam Baker in a swimsuit! One day a bus drew up outside the school; we boys got on, and we were driven to a pool some miles away. (The girls went to a different pool, alas.) So we changed into our bathing costumes, stood around with dirty feet, with our teeth chattering, and our pasty, smelly, spotty bodies shaking a bit. For some, this would be the first bath they would have had in well over a week.

Our swimming instructor came out of a door: a big man, wearing tiny bathers, with broad shoulders, displaying a chest wild with black hair. He had a very simple way to teach us how to swim. For our first lesson we had to jump in, then float to the surface. It seemed easy enough. We got into a line at right angles to somewhere near the deep end of the pool: the first boy leapt, disappeared for a moment, then emerged, flailing around a little, eventually managing to get back to the side of the pool, then scrambled out, dripping, and wrapped himself in his towel. The same thing happened with the second boy, though he was under the water for a bit longer. The swimming instructor looked very pleased with how things were going. Then it was my turn.

I jumped just like the others, and found myself at the bottom of the pool. I assumed that I would just float up to the surface, so just waited there, looking at the shifting pattern of the water above me, holding my breath as we had all been told to do. It was peculiar being down in the water, especially the acrid sting of chlorine, yet not unpleasant. However, I didn't begin to float up, and time was passing. After a while, the water above me exploded; it was the instructor diving in! He came down, scooped me up, and dragged me to the surface. I was spitting water, and my nostrils ached. He was all waving arms and wild eyes. "What you *fink* you're *doin'*?" he yelled. "I was just waitin' to float to the surface," I replied as best I could, still trying to get the water out of my nose. "As you said," I added, cautiously. "You're right daft, you are! You could've drowned down there!" he roared. "Another minute an' it would 'ave been too late!" (A pause while he collected himself, doubtless thinking of the Authorities coming round to see why a boy had died while learning how to swim, and why the first lesson was conducted near the deep end of the pool.) "You were supposed to *push* yourself *up* once you found yourself down there! Didn't you 'ave any *instinct* to do that?" he asked incredulously. There had been no talk of instincts or pushing oneself up from the bottom, only of floating up. "No, sir," I said (sullenly thinking to myself: "Just doin' what I'd been told"). "Well, go and get dressed. No more pool for you." It was a long bus ride back to the school. I hadn't been afraid down at the bottom of the pool, but thereafter I was scared of the water. My parents were shaken by the story I told them when I got home—they'd never learned to swim and kept away from any expanse of water bigger than the bath—and I was excused from swimming thereafter. I had to stay in the class and write a story, though none of them ever seems to have been read or returned to me.

Better than the swimming lesson was a class outing to the Tower of London. We had to dress neatly and were strictly told that we had to be sensible in the coach and to stay together when we were out of it. We would be seeing the crown jewels, Traitor's Gate, and learning some history. We'd already been told about the smothered princes Edward and Richard. Could anything be more captivating? Like a couple of others sitting at the back of the coach, I got motion sick on the way there. Hearing one of the boys endlessly talking about how much he wanted to see this girl or that girl naked didn't help, nor did him telling us what his Dad said about what he saw in a strip club in Soho after going to a boxing match, nor did the drawing he passed around of a naked girl (traced from an advertisement for a bra). "Wot would you take off 'er next?" he kept asking me, "Wot *next?*" I was getting sicker and sicker. Once there I didn't take in all that much. History had the smell of Thames water and old stone. I was overwhelmed and tired, just as I had been when Mum and Dad had taken me to look around the London Museum where I had walked from hall to hall, trying to find the Magna Carta, though when I eventually did I couldn't read it. No one had told me it was written in Latin and kept under glass. Disappointed, I went to the canteen with Mum and Dad and had a Lyons individual fruit pie and a weak cup of tea.

Just as I was getting numb, tired, and fed up with walking through the Tower, I saw two things, one after another: suits of armor and a chopping block. The suits of armor, complete with chain mail and with swords nearby, were endlessly fascinating, but they were made for boys. I had two questions for teacher: "Why did boys back then 'ave to wear armor?" and "Where's the armor the knights wore?" These were sensible questions, I thought, but Miss couldn't answer them. She had to consult with one of the guides who came over to me and, bending down, said in a kindly way, "Those *are* the suits of armor of the knights. Men were much shorter then than now."

This was a revelation: all those battles I had been reading about in comic books or that Dad had told me about—between Harold and William, Good King Richard and whoever he was fighting against, Lancaster and York, the English and the

French—were all with men about my height! All of a sudden, I saw the past differently; it wasn't anything like *The Adventures of Robin Hood* or anything to do with other knights that I had seen on the telly. It wasn't even like mods and rockers hoeing into one another with fists and flick knives outside the local, it was more like kids who got to clank around in armor, killing one another with swords and crossbows. Lots of the ordinary soldiers were only fifteen or sixteen in battles, I learned. Even more absorbing was an execution block that we passed, complete with a huge axe nearby. We boys gathered round, inspecting it very closely. It was hard to see anything much because everyone wanted to see, but I was assured that you could make out blood on it, and that was worth the long coach trip. The other boys walked away, eager to see the next grisly thing, but I lingered a little while and saw that the hollow where you would put your neck was just the right size for a boy of my size. Those two things suddenly brought English history into focus for me. I felt its wintry shadow. Dad had always waxed lyrical about history. Now I understood why: it was about ourselves.

Which was one reason why I wanted to learn to shoot a longbow properly; it would put me in contact with an England that, filtered through my father's stories of the past, had begun to captivate me. Another reason was my parents' feeling that I needed a hobby of some sort; it wasn't right for a boy to live so deeply within himself for so much of the day, and rambling around the streets wasn't a good thing, either. There was nowhere around Broad Street or the Heathway where one could buy a longbow, and I dare say that they would have been too expensive for my parents anyway. Mum was telling the story to a man she knew who worked in a local lumberyard, and he said he'd find a bow for me. He came across all sorts of stuff while scrounging around the East End, he said. One day, weeks later, Mum yelled out to me to come and look out the front door. The man's horse-drawn

cart was coming down Rowdowns Road, and he was standing in
the back of it, holding what seemed to be a longbow, triumphant.
As the truck started to pull up outside our house, he pulled it
hard, imitating Robin Hood, and the thing snapped in two. I
went back to my comic.

Even better than the Tower of London was the class proj-
ect we did. We had to grow some watercress. So we got an old
plastic container, peppered it with little holes, and put soil in it.
Then, very carefully, one of the girls sprinkled some seeds over
the dirt, and one of the boys watered it with a tiny watering can.
It was a sacred duty for each of us to water the cress until it was
ready. A list was drawn up and pinned next to the blackboard;
you had to tick off your name when the job was done. The first
thing we did when coming into class was to gather around the
cress, and sometimes judge whether Sammy or Ronnie had put
in too much or too little water. We all had a stake in the experiment, since our names would be put into a hat; whoever's name
was picked out would get the cress. We all desperately wanted
it. Six or seven weeks went by. Eventually, Miss declared that
the cress, now about four inches tall, was ready; she put all our
names into her hat. We all held our breath. Then she called out
my name. It seemed completely unreal. At the end of school, I
took home the wonderful container with its thick green bush.

Mum was perplexed by it. I enthused about its qualities,
which teacher had told us about time and again, and I imagine
that the experiment was approved in part to get East End kids
eating healthy green things like cress. "Wot am I supposed to do
with it?" Mum asked. "Wot did that teacher of yours say about
'ow to eat it?" That was the one thing that Miss had not said a
word about. I thought it was meant to be in a sandwich, so I but-
tered a couple of slices of bread. Then I pulled out some of the
cress, the roots of which were covered with wet dirt, and made it
into a muddy sort of sandwich. I took a bite. "Delicious!" I said,

knowing that it was meant to be. Mum looked doubtful, and when she left the kitchen, I threw it in the bin.

———— ▼ ————

I would have a piece of toast with marge or bacon fat or a shallow bowl of cornflakes for breakfast, a sandwich of thin white bread with a slice of spam for lunch, sometimes a bag of cheese and onion crisps at the Tuck Shop, then, night after night, fish fingers, fried mince, tinned peas and watery mash for dinner, or faggots (or saveloy), pease pudding and mash. In winter we had Welsh rarebit, or a stew with meatballs that sat on the stove for days getting thicker and thicker. (Dad said if we had it one more day it would walk to the table by itself.) Mum was always too busy to cook anything elaborate; Dad was either at work or sleeping upstairs. Often hunger could be assuaged by cup after cup of tea, and sometimes, if things were going well with dressmaking, with a chocolate biscuit or two. Twice a year, Christmas and Easter, we had a small roast chicken, though it was only the bird that signified something special. Going shopping down the Heathway and gazing at stuff on the shelves, I used to fantasize that we could have a Vesta curry one evening. I would come home, and there it would be, an exotic mixture of beef and vegetables surrounded by a neat circle of white rice, just as it looked on the pack! But the fantasy never materialized; the closest I got to it was a can of Heinz ravioli. We had fish 'n' chips, with a wally, wrapped up in *The News of the World*, from the Heathway two or three times a year: battered cod and hot chips all doused with salt and vinegar. At other times we bought winkles and whelks from the "Seafood Man" who came by on Friday evenings.

Once, on the Fifth of November, we were traipsing home from evening shopping, and saw a scraggy Guy in flames at the corner of the Heathway and Hedgeman's Road. Dad gave a penny for the Guy; we bought a bag of roasted chestnuts, and warmed our hands while waiting for them. The fragrance was alluring, but that first time they tasted just like dirt. I made a face, remembering the cress. "If the wind changes, it'll stay like that forever," Dad said, pointing to my ugly face. We had to build a bonfire of our own when we got home, and so we did. Once or twice we burned a Guy as well, made from leftover material and lining, stuffed with newspaper and scraps from cutting out, but always we had fireworks: crackers, pinwheels, sparklers, Catherine wheels, all sorts of skyrockets, and bangers. Dad would buy them on the way home from work, hide them in the pouch hanging on the side of his bike, and secretly carry them downstairs, locking them in the little room next to the Coal Bunker; it reeked of Esso Blue. We let them off one at a time, taking turns, though I tried to keep the rockets for myself, launching them from a jam jar, or, if they were big ones, from a bucket. The sparky night was magic, smelling of gunpowder, just as the following day was, in another way, when my mates and I would roam the empty streets, finding dead rockets sent from who knows where. ("You fink that's one of Jimmy's that came on over from Arnold Road?") Each year we heard stories of kids who had blown off a finger or two by holding a banger for too long. Yet no one ever told me who Guy Fawkes was, and why we had to burn him in effigy each and every year. And who was Catherine? I would wait many years for an answer to that unasked question. It was all part of a hunger of another sort.

Every so often we would get a bag of Jaffa oranges, tangerines, or Granny Smith apples, and I would go for them with unbounded zest. I remember looking steadily at myself in the bathroom mirror when I was eight or nine. I had cold sores at the end of each side of my mouth. My gums used to bleed, and my idle hours were spent watching white spots rise up my fingernails until they could be chewed off at night, only to be replaced by others inexorably making their way up. They were tiny alien spacecraft that had somehow got trapped inside my body and were trying to get back to their own world far away in outer space. Whenever there was fresh fruit in the house I would lunge for it. Once I had two apples in a row. "Wot on *earth* do you fink you're doin'?" Mum asked in a panic while looking up from her Singer. "They don't grow on trees, you know!" She was genuinely angry, yet she realized right away what she had said, and at the same time I knew what she meant: these things didn't come cheap.

I would go to bed after *Coronation Street* or *Hancock's Half Hour*, my sister sometime after, then my parents would retire to their dark room. All the bedrooms were freezing, since the only heater was in the living room, and I would fall asleep watching an earwig make its slow progress across the Sahara of a wall. Yet sometimes Dad had to get up for the early shift. If he did, he would have been upstairs hours before and we would have to be quiet or else. At times I would go to bed hungry. I had convinced myself that my parents and sister had *another meal*, a secret one, when I had gone to bed. I had asked Mum about this several times, and each time she had told me not to be daft. Yet one night I woke up, smelling something utterly delicious. The smell floated up the stairs; its tendrils reached into my room and wrapped themselves around my head. I got up, quietly, and ever so carefully eased myself onto the top of the stairs so that I could look down into the living room without being seen. It was true! There they were, all three of them, as bold as brass, eating freshly cooked bread pudding! In the morning, I went straight to the kitchen and saw the empty pan, with crumbs in it, and like a bobby pointed out to my mother the clear evidence of the crime. "Well, we 'ad some bread puddin' before bed," she mildly said, without the slightest sense of guilt. I was flummoxed. I realized then and there that adults could not be trusted an inch.

———— ▼ ————

The next year Fergie was to be my teacher, and I spent the summer holidays scratching the itchy prospect of a whole year with him. I had a calendar and woke up early and crossed off the day first thing so that I wouldn't get confused, miss the first day of school, and so be caned. When the new school year started, we were the big uns, which meant those of us whose parents wanted us to go to Grammar School had to study for the Eleven Plus. Childhood had been an immense plane without perspective, in which everything was present—good, bad, and indifferent—and in no particular order; the past didn't diminish the further I passed away from it, and the future didn't press on me, threatening to differ from the present. Now, approaching my final year at Thomas Arnold, all that was to change. My life started to assume a narrative shape; it was directed at something, even if it was a hurdle that might very well trip me up.

Fergie hid an immense laziness behind a patina of anger in class; he taught little or nothing. Usually, he would stand in the front of the class, all year copying a landscape by Constable in oils. His strokes were small, considered, authoritative. We did our sums or wrote a story about our holidays at Folkestone or Southend in a desultory manner; meanwhile, he pondered a hay wain in an England we would never know, no matter how far we took a Green Line bus into the country, and probably he didn't know, either. Our dads worked at Fords, at the Beckton Gasworks, down at the London docks, on the railway, in local shops if they were lucky, or they didn't work at all and sat around the house all day or wandered up and down the Heathway; and most of them, with job or without job, got to their local as quickly as they could after work. Our mums worked on assembly lines at Briggs, at the Heathway, at the Broad Street Market, or sat at home with babies and little kiddies. They went to Goresbrook Park with prams when it wasn't raining. Most of them had hard,

worn faces, inured to disappointment, yet capable of being softened by kindness. Their eyes said that the kindnesses were few
and far between, though. Mine worked in our living room at her
sewing machine day and night, running up dresses for local girls
and doing weddings.

On his easel, next to his brushes, oils, and turpentine lay Fergie's cane. Sometimes he would pick it up and stalk between
the rows of desks. He would stop behind you, looking over
your shoulder to judge the quality of your work. You'd hear him
breathing heavily; his breath smelled of tea and ginger biscuits.
Sometimes he'd poke you in the side with his cane if he wasn't
satisfied with what you were doing, or he'd rest it on your neck:
cold wood that made me sweat. I was an easy target, being left-
handed. Whenever he saw me writing with my left hand, smudg-
ing whatever I was doing, he would bring his cane down smartly
on the knuckles of that hand. *Crack!* Pain then numbness meant
that I couldn't write any more that day. "Use your *right* hand,
boy!" he shouted when he saw me just sitting there with my
hand under my bum, and I tried that, but my handwriting went
completely loopy and I gave up.

I wasn't the only object of Fergie's ire. One day he singled out
Ronnie, who always had a runny nose, for wearing female sandals. It was winter; he had very thin socks on with ragged holes
around his big toes. Fergie pointed at the sandals with his cane.
"They won't do for school, boy!" he thundered. The poor child
burst into tears, and the whole class went very quiet. In the end,
he blubbered that he had no other shoes, and that his mother
had said he had to wear his sister's sandals to school. He put
his head in his arms and lay on the desk sobbing heavily. Fergie
stood at the front of the class, at a loss, perhaps for the first time
in a long while. Then, beautifully, one of the girls, Millie Steele,
who was skinny, wore big, round NHS glasses, had long tangled
brown hair, and who we boys often tormented with jokes that

she was a witch, simply went up to him, put her arms around him and comforted him. Even Fergie relaxed a little. "You alright now?" she asked, tenderly, in no more than a whisper. But we all heard. The boy nodded, and Millie returned to her seat. His tear channels made it look as though his face had cracked.

In the final year of Thomas Arnold Primary School boys and girls had a privilege that not everyone took advantage of. We could choose not to use the London County Council pens—deeply stained wooden things, chewed at the top year in and year out, with blunt old nibs that blotted every time they were used—and bring in a pen of our own. I don't know how, but my parents bought me a brand new red Parker fountain pen, which was a pleasure to write with, and the sheer gratification of holding it made me begin to write with my right hand almost at once. It came with an elegant new bottle of blue-black ink, so I didn't have to use the wretched stuff in the inkwell on the desk, often clogged with hair, snot, and tiny lumps of torn off blotting paper that a fist of boys had put in on the way out to lunch to make the day harder for those they didn't like. How good it was to write without ink pooling around whenever I made a stroke! I would go home eagerly after school and write with my new fountain pen.

I started to compose an alphabet book based on peculiar creatures that I imagined and could draw with my pen and write about. No sooner was I away from school than I escaped into a private world, though in truth it enveloped me on many days in school as well. Not only was I cripplingly shy when outside the house, especially with adults, but also I was dreamy as well. That first fountain pen was a talisman. Thereafter, I never again held a catapult or a flick knife; never again did Fergie strike me on the knuckles of my left hand. Yet it is my left hand that remembers him best.

———▼———

Millie Steele may have looked a little like a witch, but the image at once hardened and softened in our minds when, one dress-up day, she called our bluff and raised the stakes in a way we could never have foreseen. "'ave ya seen Millie?!" a pirate excitedly asked me when I got to school. "Wait till ya do!" In the classroom there were tramps and bobbies, soldiers and Beatles (with a plastic mop of black hair), a ghost, and even a clergyman; but the sight of Millie knocked the breath out of us. She had come as a witch: she wore a pointy black hat with cobwebs falling down her back onto a black cloak, and she carried a kitchen broom in one hand and a spell book with a black cat and stars on it in the other hand. From then on, we boys all admired her. We also agreed when playing conkers at the park, after school a day or two later, that we all *liked* Millie. She had won the unkind game we had started, hands down, and had taken the whole pot. "I don't fink I'll actually *marry* 'er," one boy said tentatively, quite out of the blue, "although I always want 'er as my friend." As he said it, we weren't so sure that he hadn't become taken with her, but we were all changed enough by the experience not to say another word.

Certainly Millie was the most mature and the kindest of the girls in my class. She was also the best storyteller, as children and teacher readily acknowledged. "Sir, sir, can Millie tell us a story?" someone would call out. Then others would join in. "Yes! One of Millie's stories!" Even Fergie would relent, put down his paintbrush, sit down, and listen. With a confidence none of the rest of us had, she would step to the front of the class and then, without the slightest preparation, start spinning a tale out of nothing. They usually touched on the fantastic, and were sometimes laced with horror. Once she told us about a family that lived at the bottom of a pond in Parsloes Park; she had seen the woman disappearing into the water one Saturday afternoon with a bag of groceries. The water was the ceiling of their house; it didn't matter if it rained, and they breathed through straws so fine that passersby couldn't see them. They liked it down there, and the children played with fish and frogs; they didn't ever have to go to school. Another time she made up a frightening tale about a child that caught a Green Line bus that left London, headed north and just kept going. The windows wouldn't open, nor would any of the doors. There was only one passenger, the child, and the driver who would not turn around, no matter how often the child called out. Night started to fall, and the bus blundered on through the dark, with its headlights sweeping the road that inexorably kept pouring towards it. We were more shaken by the story than she was when she resumed her seat.

In the seat just ahead of me there sat Pamela Baker. She was almost the opposite of Millie. I don't think I ever heard her say more than "Here" when the roll was taken, but she had a preternatural calm about her that radiated in her face. Fergie always looked for her when he entered the classroom, and always smiled when she answered "Here" or "Present." She was pretty, with shoulder length brown hair, and perfectly self-contained. (On dress up day, she came as a princess, and no one made fun of her for doing so: she was simply manifesting her place in the grand scheme of things a little more clearly.) Of course, all the boys were in love with her, including me for several weeks, but there was an invisible force field around her that kept us away. If you approached her, she seemed to move herself away a mile or two; and if you were good and sat still, she seemed intensely close. Knowing this, I stayed very quiet and still in my seat, and at times she would lean back and I could smell the fragrance of her hair. When Millie was telling a story, I would sit, like other boys, with my head on my arms, as though about to fall asleep, and sometimes Pam would tilt back on her chair, and they were among the best moments of my life at Thomas Arnold Primary School.

——— ▼ ———

I was in our backyard the summer before I had to go into Fergie's class, and the neighbor two doors down, a very old man whose wife had died a year or so before (and who since then had been eating cans of dog food, Mum said), came up to the narrow bit of his garden that was close to ours and yelled out to me. "Oh, they'll *cane* yer when you go there. You wait an' see!" I could almost see his dark yellow teeth within his crooked smile. I wasn't doing anything bad at the time, though my friends and I had tormented him by playing "Knock Down Ginger" on his front door once or twice a week for months. I was standing by myself now, though, and, of all things, planting bulbs. I had implored my Dad to let me have a foot or two of dirt in our skinny back garden, usually filled with flapping washing left for hours to dry in the drizzle, to grow something. My favorite flower, then as now, was the tulip, which I must have read about in a library book, and for some unfathomable reason I wanted to grow black tulips.

One Saturday morning when walking down Broad Street, my father and I went into a shop, looked around and found nothing but seeds for daffodils, roses, and other flowers and vegetables, but then my father, bless him, went up to the desk and ordered some bulbs for black tulips. A few weeks later they came into the shop, so I cleared a couple of feet of earth to the right of the shed and planted them. I was imitating my grandfather who talked on the weekend of his allotment at Becontree, where he grew all sorts of vegetables and extolled the virtue of pig shit as a fertilizer. Well as maybe, but *I* would grow *black tulips*. Perhaps my father had said just that to our old neighbor, and it was what had made him cross. Or maybe he simply remembered the evenings when his front door knocker was rapped time and again, dragging him away from the idiot box, his only comfort these days. I retreated into the house after he called out to me. I had got the idea that he had told the teachers there to cane me. But caning would not be the worst thing about the place. It would be a steady combination of the fear of being caned, kneed in the stomach by a male teacher, slippered with a plimsoll, slapped on the arm or hit on the hand with a ruler by a female teacher, kept in after school, or merely told off in an inexplicable explosion of temper, and, even worse, the sense of time turned to mud by problems I couldn't do, a grueling sense of hours slowly leaking little ticks and tocks until a bell would finally go off in someone's hand. Then, on the way out, there would be "bundles," fights between boys that had been threatened at times during the day, mostly out of boredom, and that had simmered all afternoon—"You 'ear? It's on! Gonna be a bundle between Mike an' Ronnie after school!"—but which were sometimes abandoned because mothers in head scarfs were waiting for us at the gate, usually with prams before them, fags hanging out of their mouths.

The one bit of the week I looked forward to at school was "reading," which mostly meant listening to a teacher read a chapter or two from the King James Version of the Bible. The best times were listening to a BBC performance of John Bunyan's *The Pilgrim's Progress*. Of this I am sure: the only moments at Thomas Arnold Primary School when I was not afraid or bored were during "reading" or hearing one of Millie's stories. In truth, I had next to no idea of the biblical stories that were being read to me, but they touched me in a very deep place, and the reading of Bunyan's densely populated, immense story, week after week, made a profound impression on me, not least of all because of the BBC actor who read them. Surely God would speak like that! When the teacher took over, to complete the book, it was less impressive, but the story remained astounding. These lessons, such as they were, lasted only twenty minutes at most; and yet they made me long for more. Bunyan's allegory flexed in and out as I listened with my head down on my arms, the characters as real as the generations of penknife carvings of smut I saw day after day on that desk.

Bunyan spoke of the narrow way that Christian had to take; it "lay at the bottom of the Hill (and the name of the going up the side of the Hill is called Difficulty)." He climbed and climbed. Other characters came into the story and its continuation, and their names and language sank into me. "*Valiant-for-Truth*: I am of Dark-Land, for there I was born, and there my father and mother are still." Bunyan might well have been talking about an expanse of wasteland I would visit on weekends on my bike with a friend or two and which I would leave only as the sun was going down. He might have been talking of our dark council house near the school or the entire grimy part of London in which we lived, except for the fact that there was no one remotely like Valiant around, except in the comic books I would read.

A year before we got a TV on the Never Never, I would read in the late afternoon *The Little Engine That Could*, which resonated with *The Pilgrim's Progress* in some ways. A little train would climb a hill with a high gradient that other, bigger engines would avoid and would say to himself, when the hill seemed steep, "I *think* I can, I *think* I can, I *think* I can," and, when at the top, would triumphantly declare, "I *thought* I could!" The moral lessons from school and the story were at once felt intensely then forgotten completely in the schoolyard, although they were always reinforced when my parents would say before I had a test at school, "Always do the best you can!" It was said in a tone long accustomed to disappointment, since they both knew deep down that my "best" would never be very good. Far more pleasurable than *The Little Engine That Could*, though, was *Ivor the Engine*, which I started to watch a bit later, and which had far less of a moral and far more of Ivor's longing and occasional mild mischief, like running off by himself to the beach.

What I loved about *Ivor the Engine* was the poetry of its characters: Jones the Steam, Evans the Song, Dai Station, Mr. Dinwiddy, a crazy old miner, and—a wonderful touch—Idris the Red Welsh Dragon who sometimes sang "Land of my Fathers" in the local choir. Ivor's great longing was to sing in the Grumbly and District Choral Society, which seemed endlessly more attractive than belting out the morning hymns at Thomas Arnold Primary School down the road. For a start, the Welsh could sing in tune and had a religious passion completely unknown in my East End. Enchanted, I heard them in the tiny chapel with Ivor. My mother had worked briefly in Wales, in a little town called Mountain Ash, northeast of Cardiff; she recalled life there very fondly and would look on indulgently at Jones the Steam and Ivor's small adventures every now and again when changing a bobbin or feeding new material into her Singer while I sat, leaning towards the screen, relishing every moment.

Ivor was wildly different from the stories I would hear on Saturday afternoons at my grandparents' in a council house in a banjo on the Becontree Estate. They were almost always about British Rail at the London Docks. My grandfather operated a crane or a derrick for them all his working life, apart from some years in the army during the War. He got his gold watch when the docks had to change in order to deal with containerized cargo; the new ships simply couldn't get down the Thames as far as the dock where he worked. So all I heard over those heavy lunches of kidney pudding, lumpy mashed potatoes, furiously boiled cabbage, or marrow baked into submission were stories of decline and disruption. "Bloody work-to-rule," he'd say, "bloody Jack Dash, lazy buggers those Communists, the lot o' 'em, always wantin' to strike about this or that." The only sparkle in my grandfather's life that I could see was when he spoke of being in the army in Egypt. He would show me little mementos of his time there: strange coins with Arabic letters, little black

wooden statues of natives with tight golden rings around their
necks, small leather wallets smelling of old bazaars. Photographs of him around Cairo in his sergeant's uniform show him
to be strong, confident, and happy. He was in his element. And
so was Oliver Postgate who wrote the scripts for *Ivor*. Only many
years later did I realize that he had been strongly influenced by
the poetry of Dylan Thomas, and especially by his play, *Under
Milk Wood*. I would not read either of them until I was a teenager
in Brisbane; and when I did, after having read P. B. Shelley, T. S.
Eliot, and G. M. Hopkins in my bed at night, they seemed, like
those other poems, more real to me than my own life. So there
was a hidden track that went from the world of the railway, real
and imaginary, to reading and writing poetry.

Maybe there was another hidden track as well. In retirement
my grandfather lived in order to escape to his little shed in the
back garden where he would heap hour upon hour doing woodwork. He was an accomplished carpenter, having made, stained,
and French polished all the furniture in his house, some of it in
walnut. To my eyes it seemed utterly flawless. ("Lovely bit of
furniture 'ere, Jim," relations would always say on one of those
rare, stiff occasions when they were over for tea.) There was
even a grandfather clock, of which he was very proud. We didn't
have one at home. I supposed that you had to be a grandfather
before you were allowed to have one in the house.

Sometimes, when we were visiting on the weekend, I would
go to watch him working in that shed made of bits and pieces
of leftover wood and corrugated iron that he had scrounged
from the estate. It was dark inside, smelled of oil, blond curls of
wood, and had sawdust on the floor; it was lit only by gaps in the
wood, iron, and glints from saws of different lengths and with
varying grades of teeth hanging from the wall, from hammers,
nails, from planes, files, and the vise. He was patience itself as he
worked steadily, sawing or planing or sanding, not appreciating

any questions posed by his grandson, and breathing through his pipe. He and the pipe were one; he would smoke it in bed (where he once set the sheets alight), in the bath, and on the throne, only reluctantly putting it on the dining table during dinner. His round tin of Dunhill Navy Roll entranced me; I loved the sweet peppery smell. He wore away two teeth where the pipe stem would be lodged in his mouth. And he would talk without taking the pipe from its slot. Nan, though, hated the pipe. "Bloody well smokin' away all yer money!" she exclaimed one afternoon. "I could've 'ad a nice new carpet 'ere, but it's all gone up in soddin' smoke!" Once Granddad got embers from his pipe on his shirt, and they burned right through. "Who d'ya think's gonna mend *that*?" Nan said shrilly. "Getaway with ya," Granddad said, "makes it better that way." He winked at me.

After a while, I would leave him to his smoking and his woodwork, since it could be risky to overstay my welcome in his shed. Even in his sixties he was like an alarm clock that could savagely go off, but no one knew the day or the hour. So I'd go indoors, watch TV, and have a cup of tea and a cheesecake that Nan had bought specially for me at the Becontree shops, or join her chasing after a chicken with an axe in her hand. Sometimes she would cut off a chicken's head; it would still run madly around the garden, drops of blood flying around, and her in her apron in hot pursuit. "Come 'ere, you bloody fing!" she would shout at it, its head and an inch of neck still in her hand, blood flecks all over her apron. Or I would go out into the banjo to see if any kids were playing there. If the street were empty, I'd sometimes go to the police box over the road; it was the TARDIS just landed. But what would the Daleks be doing in Becontree in 1963 or '64? Plenty: they might even be hiding behind the bakery on Gale Street.

Even though I wasn't allowed to slouch around the shack for long, I was awed by the way in which my grandfather used skill to turn time into beautiful objects, and even as a child I realized that the same gene had passed to my mother the dressmaker. Years later at Eastbrook when I had to learn woodwork it was immediately apparent that I had not inherited the gene. "Now boys," the woodwork teacher started, "today we're going to learn how to do mortise and tenon joints." (He paused richly.) "Fundamentally," he went on, "it's just like sex." (We were eleven years old.) My exercise in making a mortise and tenon joint resulted in a hat peg that collapsed as soon as my father put his cap on it. Things only got worse, but I was to find that I could develop another sort of craft. I could only hope that sex, of which I had a vague idea from pictures avidly passed around in the school toilets, would be better.

At first, that other craft was cooking. As a little boy in London I used to watch my mother preparing stews, baking a jam roly-poly, mixing up a tin of bread pudding, and steaming spotted dick wrapped in a tea towel. Every so often she would let me do the washing up, then I graduated to helping her cook. After a while, I could have the kitchen to myself. My initiation exercise was making rock cakes; it was very difficult to do anything wrong with these, and the result was not too bad. I graduated to simple cakes, then pies, sponges, dense fruitcake (which my father loved), and I learned the rudiments of decorating them with marzipan fruits, butter icing, or royal icing, and piping wavy lines around the edges and flowers on top. In time I started to read my comic books less and less often; instead, I would take one or another of my mother's cook books, especially one that had large black and white photographs of decorated cakes, and imagine myself a pastry chef in a London hotel. Years later, I developed the conviction that, no matter what else it is, poetry is always a craft, and I owe my sense of craft to my grandfather and mother. The gene appeared in cutting out patterns for dresses and in following recipes for cakes before it appeared in arranging the sights and sounds of language so that they could create a complex of thought and feeling and strangely intensify it before the words actually come upon the page.

—— ▼ ——

Mum had taught me to read before I went to school. I would sit by her shapely black Singer; she would read aloud the little sentences about Dick, Jane, and Spot in a thin illustrated book and I would repeat them; then she would sew for a few more minutes. Then back to the book. One day, a door suddenly opened: I could read without her help! And so I entered myself. I found next to nothing there, no stories at all, or none that meant anything to me at the time. There were hardly any books at home, only some tatty copies of *Reader's Digest*, nothing suitable for a four year old, and I had to wait until school before there was something called "reading." Once I got there, we were not allowed to borrow from the small school library, and only rarely allowed into it. Once I was allowed to borrow and take home an illustrated book of *Sinbad the Sailor*. Another time it was *The Wonderful Wizard of Oz*, which I read almost in a trance and, as I did, identified now with Tin Man, now with Lion, and now with Scarecrow as they advanced along the Yellow Brick Road towards the Emerald City. I wanted more, but visiting the library at lunchtime and after school was for "higher grades," though when I got into the highest grade nothing changed.

I kept pestering my parents that I wanted to read more books about Doctor Dolittle. I had heard the first volume read in school and I wanted more. So I was taken to join the local library, the first time anyone in the family had ever done so. It was in Church Elm Lane, a good mile and a half away from our house. My dad took me there of an evening when he was on day shift, the icy air nipping my cheeks as we stepped along, each swaddled in a woolly, scarf and duffle-coat. My library card: how clean and stiff it was! How neatly the name "Kevin John Hart" was written in blue-black ink! Terrified of the librarian, a woman whose face was all wrinkles and glasses but no mouth— she had a thick sweetish smell and bony hands—I looked down at my feet when she muttered what I had to do. I misread the sign over her desk, and thought that I *had* to read four books every two weeks (rather than that I could take out at most four books every two weeks), and so I did as I was told. I would find one book, then a second; a third would take me longer; and a fourth—sometimes I had to grab one in a hurry, and often it was far too demanding for me. It was getting bitter outside, looked like rain, and Dad wanted to go home. I read them all, sometimes trying even the harder ones, partly out of fear that the librarian would question me about them in one of those small dark rooms behind her desk. I wanted to read Doctor Dolittle, picture books about dinosaurs and talking animals, illustrated stories from the *Arabian Nights*, but ended up reading all sorts of other things as well: books plucked from a shelf because my father was tired of waiting and wanted the warmth of the paraffin heater at home.

——— ▼ ———

"Blimey, look at 'im! 'e's all 'oly now," my sister said one night when I had found my father's copy of the Bible and brought it downstairs in the warm to read. I wasn't, no more than any other kid on the block who played "Knock Down Ginger" of an eve-ning, had a peashooter, a flick knife, a homemade catapult and a decent hidden supply of staples, battered marbles, and stones to go with it, but I wanted to read more of those stories I had heard at school. Now that my father is dead, I have the same Bible before me, small, broken-backed, with tiny print, and the smell is just the same. It's the odor of Moses on Mount Sinai, the smell of smoke:

And it came to pass on the third day in the morning, that there were thunders and lightnings, and a thick cloud upon the mount, and the voice of the trumpet exceeding loud; so that all the people that *was* in the camp trembled.

And Moses brought forth the people out of the camp to meet with God; and they stood at the nether part of the mount.

And mount Sinai was altogether on a smoke, because the LORD descended upon it in fire: and the smoke thereof ascended as the smoke of a furnace, and the whole mount quaked greatly.

And when the voice of the trumpet sounded long, and waxed louder and louder, Moses spake, and God answered him by a voice.

And the LORD came down upon mount Sinai, on the top of the mount: and the LORD called Moses *up* to the top of the mount; and Moses went up. (Exod. 19: 16–20)

That's what I read, slowly, hesitantly, with little or no understanding, while the TV was glaring and blaring at no one in particular, my mother busy at her Singer and my sister doing her homework on her lap. It was the Bible my father was given when he was confirmed at St. Edward's Sunday School, Romford, in the Advent of 1929 when he was eleven years old.

"Leave 'im *alone*," Mum said, distractedly, out of the side of her mouth, her fag hardly moving there, her ashtray full, and went back to her sewing. She was always working, head bent down over her old black Singer smelling of machine oil, with pins, safety pins, French chalk, elastic, tape measure, and lace scissors all laid out nearby. (Her pinking shears made me think

of an alligator I had seen in a comic book.) A bride and her
bridesmaids would be coming soon, tomorrow or the day after.
It was always the same: a bride would be coming for a measur-
ing, a fitting or a collection, and there was work to be done.

———— ▼ ————

I knew what was forbidden in those days: my sister's set of encyclopedias. There were twelve or thirteen volumes—slim, hard-
backed, gleaming, and smelling of glue. A man had come to the
front door some weeks before and talked my reluctant mother

Pauline

into buying them. Truth be told, we'd have to tighten our belts
a notch or two so as to afford them. But the salesman knew just
what to say, "Missis, you buy these, an' your daugh'er'll do well,"
he said, beaming into her face, adding, "Worth a *small* sacrifice,
ain't it?" A few of the volumes had mathematical or scientific
symbols on them. I imagined that they were part of my sister's
world, for she was going to George Green's Grammar School,
Poplar, not all that far from Charing Cross, and since she was
the first in the street to go to grammar school, I understood that

it was a very great thing indeed, the single biggest thing that had ever happened in the family. One bit of evidence was that John Betjeman once spoke at a speech night there; the teachers were taken aback when he was sitting on the stage to see that his jacket was louchely lined with dark red silk. That was my first intelligence of a poet, and it might as well have been written in one of the volumes of the encyclopedia.

I never saw Pauline pick up one of those encyclopedia volumes: she would do her homework on the Red Line bus from the Heathway to the school, or at home on the settee while watching TV and talking with Mum. She was learning French and German, and had a wonderful ear for the languages, especially French; it seemed to pass from the teacher's mouth into her brain, mouth, and hands at the same time. To me it seemed like magic; to her, very little. We could not have been more different; I was completely hopeless at school. Yet every so often, usually when I had no comic to read, I would sneak a volume of those encyclopedias away to my room, and do my best to read it. Usually I got nowhere, except for entries about history. I got my first glimpses of the Greeks and Romans under the sheets late at night with a torch. I knew what "carnal knowledge" meant: pressing a chill, secretly borrowed volume of an encyclopedia hard against your stomach so that your mother doesn't see it when she comes to say goodnight.

And I knew what was allowed; it was being in the living room when my mother had local girls, often brides and bridesmaids, come to be measured, to be fitted, and to pick up their dresses. I could be there; my father could not. If he was home, he had to sit in the freezing kitchen, read the newspaper and eat bread and dripping for dinner. Often, though, he was doing night work at the Beckton Gas Works. He slept upstairs in their bedroom during the day and was off to work by four in the afternoon, getting on his bicycle not long after I got home. My mother and father seemed not to coincide in our small dark house, save holidays and some weekends. Home was a feminine world, apart from the cat and dog, both neutered—and so I was the true exception.

— ▼ —

The Second World War always flickered in the minds of my friends and I. The East End had been bombed heavily, the main targets being the Ford Works, May and Baker (a chemical company), the Briggs Pressing Plant, and of course the London docks. But targets were often missed; in any case strategic bombing targeted where factory workers lived. So bombs fell on the Heathway, Downing Road, Rowdowns Road, and Broad Street. Many houses were reduced to rubble, and people were rendered suddenly homeless; others, whose houses were untouched, lost electricity, gas, and water; and many men, women, and children, were maimed or killed. You'd see men and women walking with a cane because one or another leg had been broken by an explosion. A German pilot, flying over our part of the East End, was shot down one night late in the war, and, so Nan told me, before the Authorities could get to him, locals had found him, tangled in his parachute and hanging from a tree, and had beaten him to death in wild fury. They ran out of their houses with hammers, chisels, screw drivers, rolling pins, brooms, knives, anything they could lay their hands on: not just men but women, too. "Soddin' doodle bombs," Nan said. "Scared the livin' shit out of us down in the tube," she said to the grown-ups, her hand cupped around one side of her mouth to hide the swear word from innocent ears but to no effect whatsoever. My father had seen a Messerschmitt hit by flak over London, remembered how it burst into flames, like fireworks, and how it inevitably plummeted out of sight. It was, he said, the most beautiful thing he had ever seen, teaching me, at a very early age, how aesthetic judgments come far more promptly than moral judgments. Every family had stories about hearing the siren, seeing flares, running down to the local tube station during the Blitz, about collecting shrapnel (some still had boxes of the stuff, which were brought out to be admired from time to time), or even finding unexploded bombs.

Kevin, Eddie, and I all had collections of toy guns; we formed what we called "The War Club," our field of operations mostly being confined to Goresbrook Park. We never were able to play fighting the Germans because none of us, and no one we could find, wanted to be a German soldier. So our games were restricted to imagining ourselves having been parachuted into occupied France. Kevin and Eddie blew up bridges and sniped at Germans who remained obstinately hidden, and I mostly stood there or lay face down in the grass, feeling it all. After half an hour or so of their successful soldiering we sang,

> *We won the War*
> *In Nineteen Forty-Four*
> *And all we had*
> *Was an apple core!*

Dad had served in France for all of three weeks, and was very quiet about it. Only a couple of times did he tell me much of what went on during his training or when he was shipped overseas. One story he would tell was when his sergeant had them on parade and asked, "Anyone 'ere who likes music, one step forward!" Dad and his mate had the same idea: they'd get off drill. So they stepped forward. "Alright, 'art and Rogers go move the piano to the back of the mess hall!" He had volunteered for parachute training one day, and then, having got back to his bunk, realized what he had done and immediately returned and crossed his name off the list. In a rash moment he had forgotten he was scared of heights.

In Normandy his unit had to secure a small village. They were standing behind the sidewall of a house, and their sergeant ordered them to run across the road. "I saw the man ahead of me start to run," Dad said, "an' saw 'is body go one way an' 'is head anovver." He threw up, and a sniper in a tree shot him in the thigh; he was sent back to England. (He showed me the wound just once, years later: a mucky hole that had sucked in flesh all around it.) Only once did he show me his medals, which he kept next to the photograph album, the dry sherry, whiskey, and rum, all kept for "special occasions" that never came. There was nothing good to say about war, he felt, and he must have quietly disliked my friends and I turning it into stories of cocky boyish adventure. The only thing that seemed to have consoled him about his years of service was that he never actually had to kill anyone. Whenever there was a storm, he couldn't sleep. Thunder and lightning brought back the War to him in all its menace, and on Guy Fawkes Night he sometimes went indoors for a while, sitting by himself in the dark.

——— ▼ ———

My parents took me to the pictures on the Heathway for the first time. We saw *Mary Poppins*. I don't know which was the more enjoyable at the time, watching the film or being in the theater. You walked into a soft darkness and, when your eyes adjusted, saw dark velvet curtains drawn across a stage, and a few black shapes sitting in the rows of chairs covered with dark plush. A girl with a stick of dusty yellow light showed us to our seats, which you could tilt back a little way; soon enough the film started, or, rather, the shorts started, and were followed by the main attraction. Throughout, the smell of Woodbines wafted over the theater; clouds of smoke could sometimes make the film hard to see. The whole ache of school, and what life would be after it, was bracketed for a couple of hours, by the fantasy of the movie, and in the interval by the girl coming round selling sweets and ice cream. Dad bought me a slab of vanilla ice cream between two wafers, always difficult to eat, and especially so in the dark. After a while the wafer got soggy or the ice cream would slide off it. You had to bite into the ice cream, which hurt your teeth. (Dad had a choc-ice, which looked much better.) Afterwards, walking home, I asked Mum what she thought of the film. "Not much," she said. Dad wasn't impressed, either. "People just don't burst into song like that, do they?" "Nah, load of old Trollope."

Thereafter I was allowed to go to the pictures on Saturday afternoons with friends. Kevin, Eddie, and I went to see *The Alamo*, which must have taken several years to make its way from America to England and then to find the little theater on the Heathway. I knew not a thing about the thirteen-day battle in which the Texans were asserting their rights as citizens of Mexico, and I doubt that my friends did, either; we all sat, close to the screen, and let the film wash over us: a great tumble of huge faces, heroic deeds, and the lyricism of "The Green Leaves of Summer." It was indeed good to be young! The film seemed to end too early for Eddie and Kevin. "Let's see a few more fights," Eddie said, so we sat there as the film began again (but there were none at all in the first hour and a half). After a while, I got bored with it and was getting hungry, but neither Kevin nor Eddie wanted to leave. It was always "Just one more battle!" In the darkness time seemed to move more slowly; it was hard to imagine that the Heathway was still outside. Surely we'd walk through the doors into Texas! Then, as the movie was finishing for the second time, a torch shone directly on my face. It was an usher with my father standing beside her. Worried about what might have happened to me, he came looking for me, and we walked back home together in silence. Eventually, I was allowed to see other pictures that came our way, and they started to

compete with our days wandering around in parks and wasteland. It was better to be entertained, we seemed to think, than to
entertain ourselves. Ever so slowly the world was changing, and
ever so quietly pulling us along with it, as though by a single hair.

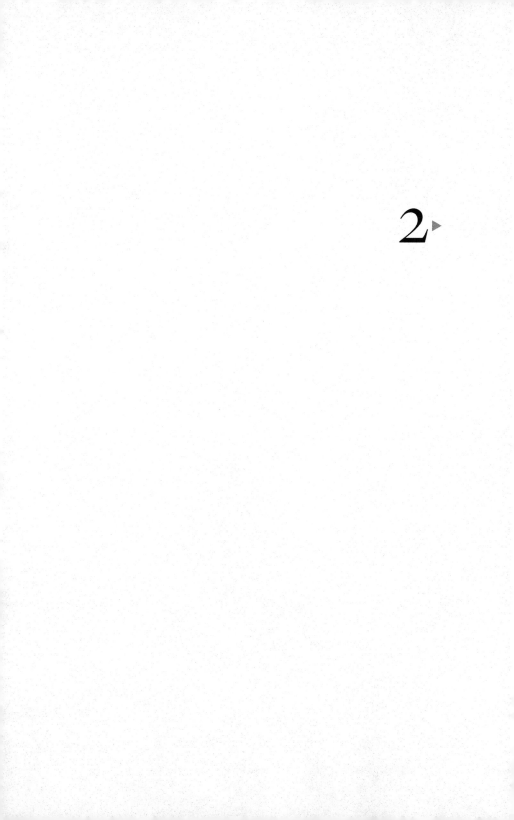

2

One day the world changed forever: a Wimpy Bar opened on the Heathway. We knew what it would be and that it would be opening before long, and for weeks we were half sick with anticipation. Little knots of people would stand outside the shop and *ooh!* and *ah!* as it was being refurbished. Then one day it was well and truly doing business. I walked past it with my friends on our way to the pictures, and we all gazed at the bright images of the wonderful things on offer and then peeked inside with longing. We had never had a hamburger, and we all craved a Wimpy Burger, though it had to be said that a Torpedo looked good as well. (A Torpedo was a ham and sardine roll; it was something for those not quite ready to take a decisive step into the brave new world of hamburgers.)

One thing that distinguished the Wimpy Bar from the rest of the shops on the Heathway was its cleanliness. It was not just clean—some shops nearby were a bit scruffy, though none was dirty—the new Lino and the white surfaces *gleamed*. The window twinkled; the electric sign glitzed. Another noticeable thing about it was what I would learn to call its modernity. Everything was straight lines, Formica, and plastic. Small as it was, it was more of a space than a place. The chicken 'n' chips shop that had opened nearby the previous year didn't keep you waiting all that long, but the service at Wimpy's was *fast*. We saw people go in and come out at a ready clip, and the little packages they were carrying had a smell like no other: warm, tasty, new, *American*. Older kids emerged with ice cream cornets in which the soft serve was swirled up into a sharp point, unlike anything you could buy at the local pictures. Now you didn't have to wait for "Greensleeves" to float down the street and then see the Wall's van turn round the corner in order to get a cornet; besides, the ice cream man didn't have soft serve then, only blocks of ice cream between wafers or a mound of ice cream shoved into a cornet. Yet when the "99" came a little later—swirled soft serve sporting a flake bar set at a jaunty angle—that was hard to beat, and so the Walls van was rehabilitated in our eyes.

As we stood there, intently looking through the window, that chicken 'n' chips place that only recently had seemed so new (how fancy it had been to have *chicken* 'n' chips rather than *fish* 'n' chips!) slid inexorably into the past. It was as old-fashioned as a Haywood's pickled onion in yesterday's newspaper damp with vinegar. A whole part of my life was vanishing as I looked. Swiftly fading, in particular, was the Lyons Corner House on Tottenham Court Road where Mum and Dad would take me for a cup of tea on their rare trips to London. Once it had seemed so posh, and even admiring its creamy cakes and finely embroidered chocolates without having any to sample had been the high point of an entire day's outing; now everything there quietly stepped back into the past. All of a sudden it was faded grandeur with its dark wood, worn velvet plush, big mirrors with dull spots, tarnished metal, and waitresses who looked as though they might have worked for Queen Victoria.

Back home, I implored Dad to take me to Wimpy's; it was everything good in the world condensed into one little shop! And just down the road! He hummed and hawed, deferred the visit, and then, one afternoon when he had a day off we were walking down the Heathway, and he said that I could go in and get something. My heart leapt up, and I opened the door into the New World. The tabletops sparkled; the ashtrays had no ash in them; a ventilator hummed; the plastic tomato had no blobs of sauce at the top; the waitresses were local girls we'd seen at the pictures with their boys, but in their new, freshly ironed uniforms, and with their hair pinned back, they looked as though they had been transformed overnight into girls whose pictures you might see in the paper. When the cashier took your order there was a slight distance in her voice, which was absolutely new. Usually, you would be called *luv* or *darlin'* at the counter but here, at Wimpy's, there was no familiarity.

A girl who came to Mum's to have dresses made was working there. She smiled at Dad and me, but her little smile was almost conspiratorial: our tacit understanding was that we knew that her job required her not to chat at the register. The experience was so freighted with significance that I hardly tasted the Wimpy burger. Their advertising image was entirely right. I was consuming the word and concept *Wimpy* in a bun; it was my first taste of American modernity, and I savored it, and as I did I vaguely saw British post-War austerity recede into the distance like the white dot when the TV stopped broadcasting late at night. The following Monday at school, once I'd poured the ink into the inkwells, I stood at the back of the room and gazed at America on an ancient map of the world that looked as though it had been rolled up for twenty years. All the States had different colors and I drooled over it for a few minutes, taking in some of the names of the cities—Chattanooga, Tuscaloosa, Tallahassee. . . —while strains of "Morning 'as bro-ken" floated into the room.

———▾———

And then the world changed again, though not forever. It was 1964, I was ten, there was to be a General Election, and by now I had a rough idea of what it would mean. It would mean that the people of Great Britain would go out to vote for the Authorities, those men in dark suits with gray hair who sat at polished desks somewhere near Big Ben and went to their clubs in the evening. My world was divided very firmly into "us" and "them"; they were the Authorities and "we" were the Unions and the Labour Party. Politics didn't vary much from football: we supported West Ham, while other people supported Tottenham Hotspur, and a gulf was set between the twain. Yet there was a difference, for the Spurs' traveling army was just like us, in a way, but those who voted Conservative were not. Who could be in favor of the Authorities perplexed me, since everyone I knew, or had ever known, was more or less as we were: living in council houses, getting by, sometimes scraping by, and content with our lot, except when there were threats of being laid off. And the Authorities kept everything for themselves. Yet there must have been people, lots of them, neighbors included, who voted Conservative. Maybe "we," or some of us at least, secretly needed them. I had, I thought, a pretty fair idea of what the Authorities were like, since my parents and my grandparents were in perfect agreement about them.

"They" had posh accents that they got from going to public schools and then up to Cambridge or Oxford, and we had working-class accents we got from living where we did. "They" played polo or rugger, while "we" played football. "They" belonged to gentleman's clubs, and ate at the Ritz; "we" had fish 'n' chips and went to the local to play darts and eat crisps. "They" drank gin and tonics (whatever they were), while "we" drank beer (I knew what that was). "They" were officers in any war, and "we" were foot soldiers. "They" knew the Queen; we steered clear of the Bobby whenever he came our way. I never saw any of the Authorities, except later when I met Harold Macmillan, and it seemed incredible that "they" could ever be ousted from the Government. They *were* the Government! They were brought up to govern; they expected to govern; and chances were that they would always govern. They were friends with the Queen, after all, and for some mysterious reason she was in charge of everything. My granddad would quote Macmillan with a sneer: "You've never 'ad it so good!" "Fat lot 'e'd know about it," he'd say, a smile starting to surround his pipe stem. "I'd like to see 'im say that load of old codswallop down at the docks an' see wot'd 'appen." And everyone would laugh.

I had seen photographs of the Conservative leader in the *Daily Mail*, the man who had replaced Harold Macmillan. His name was Alec Douglas-Home. "Wot's he need two surnames for?" I asked Dad one Saturday morning over breakfast. "Dunno," he said, "S'pose they've lots to give away where 'e comes from." (Pause.) "Toffee-nosed chinless wonder." "Who do we want to win?" "'arold Wilson," Dad said. I had seen a photograph of him as well: a kindly looking man with a pipe jutting out the side of his mouth. He might have been a distant uncle from up north who had done well for himself. When the election came it was almost as good as Guy Fawkes Night. I rushed home from school. "'ose winnin', us or them?" "Dunno yet," Mum said. But Labour won—just. Oddly enough, I imagined the Authorities to be rather relieved. Now they would have more time for polo, for riding horses, for dining at the Ritz, for sitting around in their country houses and drinking those gin and tonics. I told my theory to Granddad. "Nah, they're not pleased; they're bloody well pissed off," he said. "Ain't seen the last of that bleedin' lot!"

———— ▼ ————

When I was ten, my sister was nearly twenty, a time when she flourished. She had left George Green's, having passed her O Levels, and became a telephone operator in London; she worked in the Continental Exchange, mostly directing calls to and from French-speaking Europe. She was good at the work, enjoyed it, and was popular in the office. On her first day she took a call, which was about bringing a dead Englishman back home from France. The relation of the deceased on the other end of the line, who had no French, needed the man in Paris to arrange for the coffin and to have metal handles affixed to it. Pauline had been taught at George Green's by a French woman, had spent weeks at a time in France and Belgium, and over there passed for a French girl, but somehow her education had sadly lacked any mention of coffins and their handles. She had to flick briskly through a thick French dictionary in the room, but had occasion to use *les poignées de cercueil* only the once in her career.

One day my parents bought a telephone for the house—heavy black Bakelite, with the number DOM 4969—and no longer had to go down to Broad Street or the Heathway and wait in line to use a Red Phone Box. "Some of those flippin' girls'll talk for 'ours once they get inside," Mum said. Very happy with the new contraption, they kept waiting for someone to call them. For days on end no one did; it was like having a new puppy that didn't bark or chase its tail. And then one afternoon the phone rang. Excited, she picked it up, and slowly said, in a voice with vowels as though just neatly ironed, "Do*min*ion 4-9-6-9." Then her face went blank. Lo and behold, it was a French woman, connected from Paris, speaking rapid French to her, which discomposed my mother who was immediately helpless but frozen, quite unable to say anything or hang up, which she knew was very bad manners. She had never imagined that unknown people from overseas would call. She knew only one sentence of French, which she ventured: *Parlez-vous français?* It was not the wisest decision. The woman started to speak more quickly! Eventually, she modulated into heavily accented English; it seemed that she wanted to sell Mum a French sewing machine, *Une Chantreuse*. "Ah Madame, it is a good *one*, you will—'ow you say?—love *it*." Mum got tangled up just letting that French woman blather on and didn't know how to end it all, and must have started to wonder if having a phone at home was such a good idea. What if strange foreigners called all the time, speaking French or

German or God knows what, and all of them trying to sell you something or the other? Then the penny dropped: "Is that *you*, Pau*line*?" she asked, and heard gales of laughter at the other end of the line.

Every few weeks Pauline went out with a new chap, and sometimes she would bring them home. Mum admired Pauline—you could see it in her face when they talked; she admired her O Levels, her fluency in French and German, her job in London, her confidence, her ability to attract nice young men, and (once the impact had dissipated) even the call from the fake Frenchwoman. Forgotten by now were the ways in which she'd torture her little brother: putting me on her big rocking horse when I was very little and scaring me half to death, then, when I was older, pinning me down on the floor and dangling her long hair in my face, which I hated, were just a couple of her favorite torments. Once, when I was quite little, and the lights went out in the tube, she whispered to me in the dark that she was the Scissor Man. I was terrified. At night, safely back home, I went to the carsey in the night and when I was inside she stood outside the door and pretended that the Scissor Man had followed us home. He had come to snip off my cock! Mum found me next morning asleep on the toilet. Yet Pauline was the only person in the family to have gone to high school, let alone a grammar school. She had a bright future ahead of her. One day she could be a supervisor at the Exchange, and if she married that polite young man from Belgium doing his military service who knows what would be in store for her? They needed translators over there, no doubt, and that would be a good job. Nearly ten years younger, I was a contrast in almost every way. If only I was more like my sister, Mum would sometimes sigh to my father when I had gone up to bed.

—— ▼ ——

Dad would cycle off to Beckton and come back from it at different times, depending on whether or not he pulled the graveyard shift. It was over somewhere between Woolwich and the Thames, and of course I never went there. I would construct it in my mind from scraps I'd overheard from my parents' talk: it was an intricate complex of long pipes, vents, valves, towers, hot smoke, steel ladders, clanging metal, sweating men with cloth caps dashing around, some swearing and some with pipe steady in mouth, and supervisors who were never happy about shift schedules or production rates. The bosses were never seen—they were all in offices off-stage, wearing white shirts and thin dark ties with tie slides, absorbed in sheets of figures—and everyone lived in their shadow. There were also the Beckton Marshes to keep in mind, what with the gypsies camped there and the Jakies, poor sods. Not good to be cycling home late. I never knew exactly what my dad did there, except that he was a shop steward, and that got him into hot water with the management more times than one. Sometimes he and my mother would talk late at night after I had been sent to bed.

But stairs have ears. Men were to be laid off at Beckton due to the discovery of enormous deposits of natural gas in the North Sea; manufactured gas just simply wouldn't be competitive for long. There was even talk that the place would be closed down, something that concerned the Union because any prospect of closure directly limited their power to seek better wages and conditions. It was a replay of the stories I had heard at my grandparents' house about the closure of some of the London docks. But my grandfather had taken his gold watch, and sat at home with his pipe and slippers all day long, or did woodwork in his little shack in the garden, while Nan swept the carpet with a stiff broom, did the washing in the tub with a dolly, put it through the mangle, kept the gas meter happy, and made her indigestible dinners. "That's it! All done!" she'd say to herself as she concluded a task, "That's it! All done!" (I would think of *The Little Engine that Could*.) My dad was only in his mid-forties. What would he do? Always worried about money, he was now mired in worry about everything under the sun, and probably everything under the moon, too.

He had been an orphan, and he and his sole sibling, Bill, had grown up in one of the Barnardo's homes in London. As a teenager, Dad had started work on a farm but lasted only a week, and then he was put to work in a pub. (When he poured his first beer, he told me, he didn't know to tilt the glass and so it came out half froth. He had no idea what to do until the old man who ordered it told him that the best way to get rid of it was to pour in whiskey. He did, and so lost his first week's pay.) Older, Bill had seen how slim his own prospects were and had left for Canada years before. He had settled in Ingersoll, a tiny town set between Toronto and London, with his wife May. What would Dad do? He would join his brother in Canada!

I went there once in 1978, after a year at Stanford University. I was traveling around North America before returning to Australia and what I thought would be the rest of my life there. The bus dropped me on the main street, which had nothing "main" about it, around lunchtime, and I went straight into the first shop to ask directions to my uncle's house. It happened to be a florist, and when I asked where to find Bill Hart the florist's face sagged. He told me that my uncle had unexpectedly passed away just a couple of days before. The florist was in charge of the flowers for the funeral. It was a long trek uphill to my aunt's house, made all the longer because of the heavy news, and when I got there I met a whole bunch of wild Canadian cousins who were genially consoling themselves. I had only drunk beer before; they taught me how to drink rye. The lesson was simple. Someone poured a lot of whiskey into a tall glass, and then you drank it.

As I got to know my Canadian relations, who were at once

kindly and exciting, I kept thinking about my parents' plan all those years ago and how, if it had come to pass, I would have had a quite different life in rural Ontario or even out in the prairies where some of my cousins lived. Fancy living in a place called Saskatchewan! It was so raw out there, I learned, that at night the oil gelled in parked cars, and tires went square at the bottom if a car was left outside for too long. My uncle had been more than happy to sponsor us, but the Canadian Government wanted only immigrants with skills; and my unskilled father didn't fit the bill. I suppose they focused only on the man of the family, since my mother was certainly highly skilled. She had learned to sew in the West End under a Court dressmaker, one of those hangovers of Edwardian London, but that had been quite a time ago, and having a little business on the side in the East End probably did not impress the clerk in Canada House on Trafalgar Square. Besides, neither of them had any French, *pas un mot*. What would Dad do? There was more and more talk about natural gas at Beckton, and the writing was already beginning to appear on the wall.

Well, there was always Australia. They wanted "ten quid migrants," my parents learned somehow, and no skills were required. It was a long way to go with no one to welcome us once we were there. Dad could get some sort of job, and Mum could run up some dresses on the side. Pauline was nearly twenty-one: would she come or stay? She decided to come, despite her Belgium boyfriend whom she loved and who had brought her over the channel to meet his family. (The two of them had driven across Belgium in a small car; the land was so flat and the wind was so strong that the car was always being pushed to the side of the road.) We all liked him, especially Mum: he had bought her a charm of the *Manneken Pis* for her bracelet, and she was tickled pink. When Kennedy's death was announced on the telly one evening, he stood up straight as a lamppost, and we all looked at him oddly. "He was a good man," he said, half apologetically. *Funny people, these foreigners*, Mum, Dad and I thought as one. Pauline said something in French, and he sat down.

We all thought that they would get married after a while, maybe once he finished his military service, and Pauline would go to live in Ostend or Brussels. But she chose to join us, if we went. It was a decision weighted with a heavy fate. For me, so hopeless at school, perhaps it would be a new start. And so this time they ventured to the Strand, and to Australia House where they talked with a suntanned young man from Adelaide who was as helpful as he could be. They brought home bright, glossy pamphlets with full-page color pictures of beaches blooming with huge umbrellas, bays of intense blue water, and men with good-natured smiles breaking up cracked faces under brown, sloping hats. "At Christmas," the man from Adelaide said, "you eat chicken salad on the beach." My parents almost swooned at the idea. But it would take a long time before they could get to that beach.

———— ▾ ————

I already knew where Australia was in the world, and I knew what color it was: medium pink. At school one day we were solemnly given very old atlases to keep in our desks, and at the start of the first class in our new subject, Geography, we were told to open them to the middle. There you saw, on a double page, the whole planet like a ball of pastry rolled out thinly. "Look at the countries that are colored pink," the teacher said, impressively. "Those places are *ours*." We each looked with three eyes, and those parts were slowly named for us: Canada, large chunks of Africa, a swath of the Middle East, India, Burma, a little patch of South America, and of course Australia and New Zealand. I'm not sure if the atlas was old or if the distinction between the Empire and the Commonwealth eluded the teacher, but it hardly mattered: we were living at the center of the world, even though the East End was tilted sharply down towards the bottom of it.

My friends and I were impressed by the lesson, though, and wending our way to Goresbrook Park after school we debated what the population of the world outside England must be. Eddie ventured a thousand, but I thought that was far too small, and countered with a million. Kevin didn't think it could be that high. (There were at least a thousand people living in our street, and none of us knew what a million was.) After all, he pointed out, some of those bigger countries had white parts with "UNEXPLORED" written on them. When my parents told me that we might be going to Australia, and told me to keep it a secret in case it didn't happen, I wondered if we would go to one of the pink parts or the white ones, and I couldn't work out which would be better. One advantage the white ones had was that it was extremely unlikely there would be schools there. We'd live in a house that we built ourselves, and have only the horizon for company. I too could have astonishing adventures in foreign parts! Mum and Dad were adamant that they didn't want to live anywhere cold again, and they settled on Brisbane as the place they would seek a new life for themselves. It was about halfway up the east coast, not as big as Sydney and warmer than either Melbourne or Sydney, and, when I checked the next morning at school, decidedly one of the pink parts.

———— ▼ ————

My father met my mother when he was strolling down the Heathway. It was a summer day during the War, and he was in uniform. "I wasn't lookin' where I was goin', and I bumped into her," he told me when I was in my late thirties and she was dead. "It was an accident," he added. It happened outside a pub—nowadays it's called the Lord Denman—and his line was a familiar one, "Oh, I'm sorry! Lemme buy you a drink." She said yes; they got married; and a fair number of years later, I was born.

When he told me the story it was the word "accident" that pierced me, and it was a day or two later when I understood why. I recalled a row with my mother when I was twelve, living in a sleepy, ragged suburb of Brisbane. I was in bed, pretending to be ill so as not to have to go to school. The class had swimming lessons, and I was mortally afraid of the water because of what had happened at Thomas Arnold, and preferred to cut myself with Mum's scissors rather than have to go. She must have known I wasn't really ill and nonetheless let me stay home, though why I cannot guess. "All right, just *today*, an' then you *'ave* to go," she said. Then, turning round, added, in a voice suddenly grown hard and sharp as flint, "Or else you'll grow up to be an *idiot*." A dart went home. She swayed heavily away down the corridor and then quickly returned, inflamed. "Oh *you—you! You* were an *accident*, you were!" I knew what the word meant, and so another dart went home.

Only recently have the two stories come to mind. I remember more about my childhood and adolescence than ever before. I know the feel of white paint over an uneven brick in the kitchen of my childhood home in London. I experience again the heavy sadness of climbing the stairs to go to bed on a Sunday evening with the concluding strains of *Coronation Street* dying away on the television. The faded red and dark green flowers of the carpet on those stairs going up to my bedroom is more vivid now that it has ever been. I smell the pots of paste we made when wallpapering the living room. I relive the desolation of lying in my bed in the dark of night and calling out in some childish distress, "*Dad!*" time after time and not hearing his feet on the stairs. Now, over sixty, I find myself at the center of a storm of feelings I have not known for more than fifty years.

Sometimes I think that my life has had two vanishing points: my father accidentally meeting my mother, and my mother telling me in anger that I was an accident. And at other times I think my life has just the one vanishing point, and it could well be labeled "Accident." The shifts between the one view and the other are rapid and mostly lived in sleep. Before my wife and I were divorced she would tell me that I cried out at night, and truth be told it probably had more to do with my childhood than with her. In the daylight hours I felt that my life was just an echo of those cries.

Some afternoons, in those few months before my wife and I separated, I sat well away from everyone in the house and closed my eyes. I entered myself. The story my father told me speaks of an infinite debt, one I can never possibly repay, but it also whispers to me that it weighs nothing, that it was merely an accident. The story my mother told me speaks of passion; it goes back to my father's story, but never ends there. It recoils, flails around, and I cannot control it. I feel absolved from all debt, utterly free; and I feel all the more indebted to my father, whose passion I surely understand. I try to imagine my mother's passion, but a barrier soon erects itself that I am tempted to call anger and that I fear is no more than a studied lack of sympathy: stale anger. Those darts that went home exiled me from home.

All children need to be loved, and I was loved. Between my sister and I there was a stillborn child. They named her Marion. Perhaps also everyone needs to believe that he or she was imagined before conception, deeply desired, longed for with a force that marks each and every feature of the body and the soul. I do not have that, and I have long known it is the one thing that I deeply want. And yet I know that each child must separate himself or herself from that image of the idolized child to be born in order to be free and able to desire on one's own account. Since there was no plan for my birth, maybe even dismay when it was clear I had been conceived, I tell myself that I am freer than others. Perhaps I have known that since I was an adolescent. If so, I suspect it is only because I have also known that this freedom cuts its figure against a massive obligation that originates in an accident: a man bumping into a woman while sauntering down the street and not looking where he was going.

—— ▼ ——

Never entirely out of mind, there is an image of my father about the time he met my mother. He is handsome, slim, smiling, and in uniform, and each time I see that photograph I think that it is the image of him that will last in eternity. If it is true that when we die we meet the people we love, I expect to see my father as I remember him before I was born. The photograph abides in a thick black album last seen in my sister's house in the outer western suburbs where Brisbane starts to become unraveled and before Ipswich starts to find itself. It was taken down from a high, dark cupboard in my parents' bedroom once every few years, and it smelled of old clothes and mothballs. I saw it when my mother died, when my father died, and a year or two ago when I visited Brisbane for the last time.

On one of the next pages of the album there is a photograph of my mother a year or so after she had met my father, a newly-wed. I have looked at it for minutes at a time, maybe longer, and yet I cannot bring her into focus as a young woman. She enters life, for me, twenty years later; and although she is overwhelmingly real for me—I hear her fat, loose breathing on my neck as I write these lines, just as I did when she would come up behind me when I was doing homework in high school, and can smell the pale pink soap she used in the shower—I know full well that she has never been as close to me as my father. I have seen images of her as a young woman, even as a little girl, and yet she does not lean out of any of those photographs; she does not claim life in her death as my father does. She was intensely present at particular moments, not always happy ones, so that for me the rest of her life belonged to someone else and not the person I loved passionately as a child, avoided as a teenager, and, finally, learned just enough from life to let her be, albeit at a carefully managed distance.

——— ▼ ———

Of all the books I have wanted, the one I can never have is the one long kept by my sister. It is that photograph album. In his last years my father and I talked on the telephone three or four times a week, and I could have asked for it and I know that he would have sent it to me. But it would have come too late. I needed to have it when I was thirteen or fourteen, when it meant everything to me, although I hardly ever looked at it: it was a forbidden book, especially in London, kept there, as I saw one day in London when I crept up to see, beside those bottles of dry sherry, whiskey, and rum, opened only at Christmas and such times, when small serves from one or another bottle were offered to my grandparents or, from time to time, to ramshackle uncles and aunts, as they called themselves, who appeared out of nowhere, chose chocolate from a big tin box of *Quality Street* or *Roses Chocolates*, and sipped from a little glass over an hour or so; it was brought out by my father solely on special occasions. There are photographs of relations who were long dead by the time I learned their names.

Among those photographs, I would find when I was grown up a black and white snap of Dominique, an *au pair* girl from Rennes of fourteen or fifteen who came to stay with us when I was ten. (How could there have been room there for her, in that small dark council house on Rowdowns Road, with its rooms like little boxes? I suppose she slept in the same room as my sister.) The image precisely captures the curve of her mouth as she said certain words in French, English, or somewhere in between. I have never needed the album for her. I have always seen her sitting in the green armchair to the right of the fire, with long bare legs and bare feet pointing to the fire. She is tired or bored; I am a little boy, a nuisance. I am throwing lumps of paper moistened with spit at her. A few minutes ago it was a game. Now she doesn't want to play. She says, "Don't, *don't!*" I am doing it because I love the way she says that word through the filter of French.

— ▼ —

Several years ago a memory surfaced. I was very small, taken out the back of a doctor's or a hospital into a room with chemical smells. The door is shut. One of the two young nurses in the room bends over to pick up something or to retrieve something from a very low drawer and I see her knickers. They are black. This is my first memory of being aroused. Could it really be so? One summer evening I ask Dad, now well into his eighties, about this on the telephone during one of our usual long, wandering conversations. He is embarrassed about it, although he is quite alone. He tells me, by way of several *wot-do-you-call-its* and *thingamies* that, when I was very little, I had to have my foreskin removed because my mother had trouble in cleaning it. One day he came home to find my mother in tears and me screaming: she could not get my foreskin replaced properly after trying to clean it and he had to do the job. A day or two later my mother told him that she had handed me over to two nurses "to 'ave 'im done."

— ▼ —

Pauline and Dominique had been pen pals, the one writing in French and the other in English, and Dominique came for only one summer. The following year another French girl came, and the year after that she brought a friend. They stayed in their room and tried to get out as rapidly and as often as they could, much to the annoyance of my mother who thought they were acting all la-di-da. They were just suffocating. At first, my parents had the idea that an *au pair* girl would help Pauline speak French more fluently and so get on, but my sister had another idea: it would help the French girl speak English better. She needed total immersion in English! The only girl of the three that I liked was Dominique. To tell the truth, I didn't like her: I *adored* her. I was ten and endlessly in love.

Dominique had good English, of the Home Counties sort, though frilled with French *r*'s, and must have found our East End accent impossible to understand, and I can't imagine that the English teacher in Rennes had ever thought to tell her of London slang, let alone rhyming slang. Rapid London English was hard enough for her at first. We met her at Victoria Station where she was just standing, looking lost, surprised that, a good student of English, she couldn't understand a word spoken. We didn't use much slang at home—"apples and pears" (stairs), "have a butcher's" (look), "use your loaf" (head), "plates of meat" (feet), and "dog and bone" (phone)—but what we used mystified Dominique. When we walked the mile and a bit down Hedgeman's Road to Amesbury Road, where my grandparents lived in a banjo, and she met them, her bafflement increased tenfold. One of five children in a poor family, Nan had left school so early that she had never really learned to read; she was able to make out most of what was written in the newspaper, though she sometimes got impatient with it, and I never saw her read anything else. When still a girl, she went into "service" in the West End, and it was in those years that she met my handsome, strong grandfather. She was the perfect foil to him, affectionate to a fault. (She would go shopping down Gale Street with their Pekingese, and carry the shopping bags home on her arms while pulling the shopping trolley with wheels that had the overfed dog comfortably sitting in it and wetly snuffling away.)

Nan, Granddad, and Kevin in London

Nan had never stepped a foot out of London, and her knowledge of the world was limited to what Granddad had told her and
what she had picked up from the newspapers and the radio. She
acted on the firm belief that all foreigners really know English
deep down, and that one has only to speak very slowly and
loudly for them to understand. "Wanna nice cup of Rosie Lee?"
she asked Dominique, who couldn't make head nor tail of the

request. "C'mon, girl," Nan continued, her voice beginning to rise, "a NICE CUP of R-O-S-I-E L-E-E!" And then, bringing out her one bent farthing of French that Granddad had remembered from his time in France, "*Comprendy-you?*" A blank look of Gallic incomprehension met my grandmother's eyes. She started to dig Dominique in the ribs, and say, ever louder, "R-O-S-I-E L-E-E!"

"Excuse me, Mrs. Wootton," Dominique answered in confusion, "I do not understand." Pauline slipped into French—*Voulez-vous une tasse de thé?*—and everything was cleared up and Dominique got a cup of tea in one of Nan's blue willow cups and a cream horn on one of her blue willow plates. That was the set she kept "for best," in a glass cupboard that also contained her collection of Toby Jugs, and the bar was set very high for that. ("You ever gonna use 'em?" I had asked Nan months before. "When the Queen Mother comes round to tea!") Then Nan began to sing, in broad East End English, and with more gusto than melody, her very own Franglais version of "*Sur le pont d'Avignon*," doing things to the French vowels that made my sister wince. "You sing that over there, do ya, girl?" she asked, "Eh? *Eh?*" (with another dig in the ribs to ensure perfect comprehension). After a few weeks, Dominique could mostly understand my Nan. It is hard to imagine the horror of her teacher back in Rennes when she returned speaking like an East Ender! At all events, we did not hear from Dominique again.

It was enough for me, more than enough, simply to sit in Dominique's presence in the living room, especially if no one else was around. Sometimes we would play cards, or just watch the telly. Sometimes she would tell me about her life in Rennes, how she ate a croissant for breakfast and sometimes a macaroon after school with a bowl of *café au lait*. She would teach me a little French: *chatte*, she said, pointing to Bobbie; *la tête*, pointing to her head; *la bouche*, pointing to her mouth. That final noun was almost too much for me: *bouche* was so much sweeter, more delicious, than *mouth*, especially because she said it as though about to kiss. I had already dreamed of her mouth more than once. Somewhere in the back of my head there was the fuzzy outline of a plan I had developed in bed at night. If we ever went to Australia, I would return after a few years, sun-bronzed and confident, with my ears magically smaller, and speaking elegant French. Dominique would not have aged, and would have been quietly waiting for me. I would easily find her in Rennes: I would get out of the train station and ask a gendarme for her (*"Je cherche une fille jolie nommée Dominique"*), and would be pointed to a charming cottage down the road. I would knock on the front door, and she would open it, smile, and warmly embrace me, then give me a "French kiss." (Exactly what that was escaped me, but I had heard of it at school, and presumably all French girls gave French kisses. It simply stood to reason.) We would get married, and I would be a pastry chef in Rennes. I would introduce the good citizens of that town to the wonders of Bakewell tart, Battenberg cake, Welsh cake, treacle tart, and mince pies, and they would immediately lose interest in *croissants, macaroons, pain au chocolat, mille-feuille*, and all the other things Dominique had told me about. I would be a huge success.

——— ▼ ———

My parents were warm and kind for the most part, though, like most adults I knew, they had bewildering moments of anger; and my mother had impressive exertions of will that seemed entirely arbitrary at the time, though now I see that they must have come from loneliness, overwork, and worry about what would become of the family. She wore out a vertebra by bending over that Singer day after day for year after year. No matter how close to them I was, though, I always felt that there was an immense barrier between them and me. Life was something scary, controlled by adults who acted strangely, keeping its secret very close to their chests. They were both intelligent but unschooled, and found it hard to talk about anything important to one another or anyone; the words just didn't come to them. They got flustered, said blunt things they must have regretted, and retreated into frustrated silence. Or they would have whole conversations over cups of tea that turned on not knowing the right word to use: "'ere, you got that wotsit 'andy?"—"Lemme look."—"No, not that thingamy, I want the *wotsit!*" At first I thought they were talking a code that only grown-ups knew, something used to keep secrets from kids, and only much later did I realize it was one of Dad's verbal tics.

The best moments of the day would come in the evening, when I was safely home from school and had had my dinner. Then came the girls to be measured, fitted, or to pick up their baby dolls, miniskirts, wiggle skirts, or A-lines. Those dresses hung from a simple cornice and often completely covered the walls. They fell to within an inch or two of the highest that Bobbie or Kim could reach up. There was never any hurry for the girls or me to leave. Sometimes their boyfriends waited outside the house, often in the cutting dark, for hours on end. Meanwhile, they sat on the settee before the paraffin in just a slip or even in knickers and bra, talking with one another, with my mother, and sometimes with me. My mother would be drawing designs for dresses on little sheets of rough white paper, or looking at cut out pictures of Mary Quant creations and trying to work out how much it would cost to do a knock off with local material from the Broad Street Market. The girls would be leafing through *Burda* or rummaging through Mum's little library of sewing patterns—Advance, Butterick, Simplicity, Vogue—all in covers a bit torn at the top and lying higgledy-piggledy in a big cardboard box. Sometimes they would talk about those boys who must have been getting wooden outside, leaning in the doorway in their drainpipe trousers and smoking cigarettes to keep warm. ("Oh, I *do* luv 'im, *ever so*," one girl said about her boyfriend to another girl while leaning a little towards her on the settee.) Once or twice the lads would go off to the local and not be there when the girls were done, which caused a fuss. The best evenings were when brides and bridesmaids would come all at once, sometimes with the mother of the bride, and then the whole evening would be taken up, and if I could keep quiet enough Mum would forget I was there and I could stay in the warm room while the girls got in and out of their huge confections, crisp and creamy like meringues, and would talk endlessly about what was to occur and, it seemed, almost everything else that might happen in life: a nice flat in Barking, Ilford, or Romford; watching the local amateur football team play at Castle Green; nights out at the Merry Fiddlers or the Chequers; the first kiddie, and then the second...

I would be sitting there in my pants and a vest, pretending to watch the telly with Bobbie on my lap, or playing with my train set, but all the while listening to the girls, who would sometimes make a lot of me. I would see them undress and be pinned up, undress, and sit down, in no hurry to get dressed again. Or they would come to approve the completed dress, which would be when my mother would inspect each and every dart or pleat, and then the girls would sit for a while and then put on their old dresses while their new one, the one they wanted for a party or a summer holiday on the coast or even for a week on the Costa Brava, was carefully wrapped up in tissue paper. There were things to learn about hanging it and ironing it and wearing it. It was an outing, after all, and some of them had come a long way and had a long way to get home. Sometimes Mum had to slip out of the room to get something or to go to the toilet, and then, every so often, a girl would talk to me, and sometimes run her fingers through my hair or down an arm and ask me about girls at school, trying to make me blush. ("Who ya gonna marry, then,

Kevin? Sorry, *I'm* taken"—laughing and digging her girlfriend in the ribs—"an' my Brian would be *very* upset!"—another dig.) It was a giggle. Once two of them sat either side of me, running their hands down my thighs. Quickly, very quickly, they taught me how to kiss, first the one and then the other. But they straightened up right away when they heard Mum coming back down the corridor. "You've been sittin' too close to the fire," she said, looking at my burning face, and packed me off to bed.

———— ▼ ————

Sometime before I was "sick," my parents had bought me a cheap electric guitar and hired someone to teach me how to play it. Mostly by overhearing the conversations of the girls who came to Mum each evening to be measured, fitted, or to collect their dresses, I had become entranced by the Beatles and the Stones, and all the other groups of the day. I was more taken with the idea of these groups than their music, most of which I hadn't heard at all. To me it meant those sweet girls, who sat on the settee next to me in knickers and bra, out at clubs having fun on Friday and Saturday nights, dancing, smoking, and drinking, and the closest I could get to their experience was having a guitar of my own. A young man, a friend of my sister's boyfriend of the day, came once a week to teach me how to play the shining red instrument. A mod, he always dressed in a natty suit and tie, had brylcreem in his fair hair, and he wore winklepickers. We sat on my bed upstairs, quite close together, and so I smelled his breath, which was foul, and I thought: Perhaps grown-ups with teeth all smell this way. (Nan and my parents all had false teeth; they had been ripped out at the dentist as soon as it was possible to do so, giving them all a horror of dentists, which was duly passed on to me until I moved to America.)

He tried to teach me how to tune the guitar, but I simply couldn't hear the difference between flat notes and high notes, no matter how intently I listened and no matter how patiently he waited for the penny to drop for me that *this* note was higher than *that* note. I would hear some sounds as thicker, others as thinner. He would ask me to try to tune it myself, and I got nowhere fast; and so he did it for me each week. He had to earn his pay one way or another, I suppose. I easily learned the chords, and could position my fingers on the frets well enough, and yet I couldn't hear what anyone with the slightest musical talent should have heard. When the guitar had been tuned for me, I could play simple pop songs such as "Pretty Woman" by Roy Orbison, either with a plectrum or by strumming chords, and when I brought the guitar to school and tried to play it kids took the mick out of me. My musical education went no further than that.

And yet the force of my desire, combined with the sheer power of the pop music culture, was such that I conceived myself a good guitarist, and that in time I could easily play in clubs like the Merry Fiddlers. Only slowly did the sheer weight of overwhelming negative evidence persuade me I was as wrong as wrong could be; it took several years. I was no George, no John, no Paul, not even an Ivor. I was more like Dad after he'd had a couple of drinks at Christmas and started to sing "Knees Up Mother Brown!" or Nan after a cup of tea with a drop of rum in it.

Meanwhile, the guitar and all that it could produce in sound, melodious or not, continued to conjure those girls who came night by night. I was growing up, and those half-naked girls started to mean a lot to me, far more than I could draw together in feelings, let alone words.

———— ▼ ————

When I was ten I wanted to be a dressmaker. The reasons were very simple. At school I had soon settled at the bottom of the class, like something heavy that had fallen in a pond and stirred up mud so that no one could see a thing. When asked to add one and one, I would write eleven, and simply not see why it should not be so. I was just bringing the two ones together. Things were no better when Cuisenaire rods were introduced; I couldn't see why numbers should have colors, got stuck on wondering why one number could be confidently identified as green while another one was self-evidently red, and then wafted away into my own little world. My parents were concerned that I could not make my way in life—they were surely right—and so my mother took charge and thought to teach me the rag trade so that I might be able to do something. Maybe there would be a niche for me in Soho or in the ready-to-wear world. After all, I had taken an interest in dresses when staying home from school, had learned how to cover buttons, and had watched girls get fitted. Mum was partly right. Dressmaking attracted me, especially the cutting out of complex patterns from *Burda* with big scissors (and, later, small electric scissors with tiny knives like the beaks of hungry baby birds) and those other fashion magazines, and even more especially being in the room with those half-dressed girls who were kind to me.

I was ten and a half years old, maybe just eleven, about to sit the Eleven Plus examination, for which I had been given no preparation, even had I been halfway smart enough and willing enough to study for it. Anyone could sit for it, and my parents had made sure that I could, even though they weren't at all hopeful that I would pass. All Fergie would do is sit those attempting the exam all together in the back left-hand corner of the classroom. If only because of that, I felt special for a few minutes. The others had no chance at all. They'd become bricklayers, construction workers, railway workers, just like their dads; the girls would marry young, and one day I'd see them pushing prams round Broad Street. To our tight little square Fergie would give faded past examination papers for us to do while the rain doodled on the window panes, the class murmured and farted around us, and he kept painting. We handed them in and that was the last we ever saw of them.

Even as I sat in that little square of privilege, it seemed infinitely unlikely I would go to a grammar school like my sister. At school I would drift through the day, hoping not to be noticed, and if I managed to get out the gate without any attention being given to me I counted it a huge success. I was free! I could come home and snatch one of my sister's encyclopedia volumes, or read one of those four books from the local library. I would enter my snow dome of a world until it was time for dinner. I was a few years too young to fantasize about those girls who came most nights and talked about the Beatles, the Rolling Stones, the Yardbirds, the Animals, Manfred Mann, even Freddie and the Dreamers, and the local clubs where they went dancing, and the posh drinks they had (a "Snowball"—Advocaat and lemonade—was a favorite, as was a Pimm's Cup), and yet I did, in an inchoate way. I preferred their company to that of most of the boys at school—except for Eddie and Kevin—with their collections of toy guns, conkers, catapults, flick knives, and even the odd crossbow, their stories of their fathers down the pub or at a club or at a West Ham game, and also to the company of the girls at school, most of who bunched together at lunchtime at the opposite end of the playground.

Not all of them, though. One time, the year before I went into Fergie's class, my mother was walking down Rowdowns Road towards our house and saw me under the school privets with a girl. She had taken me there to hug me and caress me, but as my mother approached a female teacher on playground duty saw what has happening and sped in and ripped me away from her. Warmth left me. That evening, as it happened, Benfield dropped round on his bike to see my parents. Maybe he thinks that *I* stole that money last year! Maybe he's going to talk with them about Sally in the privets! But it wasn't either of those things, and he probably didn't know about what had happened earlier that day. But he told them something far worse, at least in his eyes and theirs: "The boy doesn't know his times table. And he doesn't know how to tell the time. We can't do anything with him. You'd better take him out of school and get him an apprenticeship." It was true: I was well into my twelfth year on earth and couldn't tell the time and couldn't learn the times table, no matter how often I had chanted it with the kids at school. I knew the edges of it all right, but the middle was soft as a bog, and I never felt safe there.

There were words at home that night between my father and mother, but in the dark when I was supposed to be asleep, far earlier than usual, I could make no sense of them. The next day, after school, Mum and Dad said they would have to send me to a boarding school. I was horrified. I'd read about boarding schools in *The Boy's Own Annual* and in stories about Billy Bunter in *Valiant*. That was the last I heard of the plan, which would have been too expensive for them anyway. Then one day a week later I had to stay home from school, and Mum took me to the butchers at the Broad Street Market and asked if they would take me on as an apprentice. My life as a dressmaker had ended! No more *Burda*! No more *Vogue*! No more *girls*! We had gone to that butcher shop each Saturday morning of my life, and I knew the sawdust on the floor, the big sides of beef dripping on it, the great wet dollops of liver under glass, the sharp knives on the counter with all its bloody cuts. The butcher was huge, his arms were like fat legs of lamb, and he had tattoos all down those arms, one of them reading *Southend* and another *Gloria* inside a heart with an arrow going through it, and his two young assistants were smaller versions of him, beefy, but with no tattoos as yet. As my mother spoke to the butcher behind the counter I could see blood slowly dripping down in fat pear-shaped drops on the sawdust from a haunch of beef or mutton. Mum had said on the way there that it was a good life because you got meat to take home, and I could instantly see myself getting the fatty cuts that no one wanted to buy for dinner and living in a small drafty flat near the Broad Street Market. I would see Pat who ran the grocery shop, and get a jamboree bag and an Appeal orange drink with its slightly gritty taste every once in a while and maybe a roll of fruit pastilles or some bulls-eyes from the sweet shop. It wasn't so bad; at least it was safe. The butcher eyed me steadily, seeing a flat-chested skinny kid without any light in him, and said, "Sorry, Missus, the boy won't do," and so I went back to school the next day.

My mother bought me a cardboard clock with movable hands and told me to go up to my bedroom and learn how to tell the time. I did; it took me all of ten minutes. "You done it?" she asked when I came downstairs. I nodded. "'bout bloody time," she said, with a face made of cement. She also bought me a book that simplified how to multiply. It was very good, and I read it with interest, since I knew I had to learn. ("You'll never get by in life unless you can multiply," Mum had said mournfully.) But the boggy bit of the times table remained soft. I sank down in it whenever anyone asked me what eight sevens were or nine eights were, and never came up for air.

———— ▼ ————

There was nothing more foreign to my parents than going to a party, or a "do" as they called a wedding reception, except to host one at home. Yet that is exactly what happened one night. My sister insisted that she have a party at home, and they finally gave in. Our small council house in Rowdowns Road was hardly the place to have more than one or two people over, and yet Pauline had invited Josie, her best friend, and lots of her friends from work and from the clubs where she used to go dancing. Boys in suits and ties and girls asterisking themselves in new dresses all appeared, one after the other, on Saturday night, and my parents more or less disappeared into the wallpaper while it all happened. Someone brought a record player, and lots of people must have brought LPs, since there was music all the night, almost none of which I had heard, and all of which was glory to my ears. Boys brought bottles of beer and babycham, which was completely new to our house, and where we found the glasses for everyone I will never know. I suppose we borrowed them from our neighbors who must have been very patient, since people in our street would usually be in bed by nine thirty. We had supplied some sausage rolls and tomato sauce, and a few plates of sandwiches as dainty as we could make them. It was difficult for me to know where to be so as to take it all in: the living room had become a dance floor, packed with music, and the corridor and the kitchen were crammed with boys drinking beer. So I sat on the stairs, fairly high up, and watched the party lapping around the bottom of the staircase.

As the evening wore on, the music slowed, and couples danced more intimately, more mouth-to-mouth than cheek-to-cheek. Others got out of the house, and made out in the back garden or in the porch. There were two or three couples that never came up for air. One boy had his tongue partly outside his girl's mouth. (Was this a "French kiss," I wondered? How exactly would one do it? How would you know if your mouth and the girl's mouth would meet? Maybe the music or the beer would help when the time came. My one lesson had not been enough, and those kisses were very short.) It was way past my bedtime, but no one seemed to notice, and I saw that there were glasses with beer left here and there. This was an opportunity! Before then, I had only had a can of shandy, which was mostly lemonade in any case, and which tasted like Tizer. So this was the night

I tasted beer. I walked around the house, picking up glasses in order to take them to the kitchen where they might be washed, but they needed to be emptied first. Most had only half an inch left, but several were a quarter full. The beer had a brassy taste that I liked. Even so, I didn't need to learn that girls are more appealing than drink, yet the music and the drink made the girls all the more enticing as they swayed slowly in their boyfriends' arms. I wished I was older.

Eventually, the party thinned out, and my parents emerged from where ever they had been, and found me sitting on the stairs, desperately trying to stay awake and clearly more than a little drunk. Mum put me to bed, and I slept through most of Sunday, waking up with a headache bigger than the whole East End, by which time the house had been set to rights.

———— ▼ ————

Every so often I would find myself upstairs in the bathroom looking at myself in the mirror. It was usually when relations had called round on a Sunday afternoon, and were having tea with Mum and Dad. They were strained occasions. I had to put on a clean dicky dirt and had to be on my best behavior. One had to use "manners," as though they could be brought out of the living room glass cabinet where china and linen were kept for "best," and then cleaned and put back once everyone had left. No one in my family was a good conversationalist. Disagreeing with what anyone said was regarded as rude, and there could be no mention of politics or religion, even though everyone presumably voted Labour and everyone was nominally C. of E. (which meant that they went to church only for christenings, weddings, and funerals).

Small differences made large chasms, though, and this meant that the main topics of conversation were work and family. So at first there was talk of decline at the Gas Works, about what had happened down at the Docks, and about Mum's dressmaking. "Still runnin' up dresses, girl?" one of my older, mustier relations, who seemed to have stepped out of the early pages of the photograph album and whose connection with our tight knot of a family was very obscure to me, would ask. The question was odd, for there were dresses hanging all around the room, with darts tacked in and pleats with pins in them, and an ironing board was folded up and standing just by the door. I was never really sure what an uncle or aunt or cousin was, though my sister won everyone's admiration by knowing everyone's exact relationship with everyone else. "Smart girl, that un," someone would always say to Mum once Pauline had left the room. "She'll get on," someone would add, nodding. Pauline would always manage to leave, going over to the West End for a party or out to a local club, shortly after recalling a great-aunt or a second cousin removed twice, and that left me having to sit up straight in the overly warm room, wondering if some aunts were bigger than others or why some cousins had to be removed. What had they done? And where were they taken? (Most likely one of the Channel Islands, I told myself.) Once Pauline had left, the conversation inevitably started to converge on two topics, Cousin Albert and me.

I had never met Cousin Albert, and I had been told from time immemorial that it was because he had caught a rare Asian disease. At first it was thought to be diphtheria, a word often darkly on Mum's lips when I was a boy and had a bad cough, mostly because she had been a carrier. But tests on Albert up in London had proved otherwise. The strange thing is that he had never been further east than the Romford Market, and the consensus was that he had caught it there. "All kinds of funny fings you see 'em sellin' there," Nan would say. "It's all those bleedin' Indians, I say, Lord knows wot they brought over with 'em," an aunt would chime in. "Bloody blacks," Granddad would add, "Wot they doin' over 'ere, anyway?" "Another cup of tea?" Mum would ask, deflecting the question just a bit. "Don't put yourself out, Rose," Granddad would say. "'ow *is* Albert doin'?" an elderly relation would ask. "Well, Ruby's still lookin' after 'im," Nan would say, "and it ain't easy" (there was a pause, and she leaned forward and spoke in a hushed voice): "'e's lost all the strength in 'is arms." (Collective taking in of breath, then collective sips of tea.) "Ruby says it's only a matter of time before 'e can't use 'is legs," Nan added. "Must be 'ard for her," someone would say in a low voice, "Oh, very 'ard!" another would agree. "There she is lookin' after 'im day in day out, always in bed. Can't do a fing for 'imself." (Long pause, taking in the full weight of the situation.) Then, in a hush, "How long d'you'll fink 'e'll live then?" "'ard to say, the doctor says: could be a year, two, maybe longer." "'ard on poor Ruby, that's all I'll say," Granddad pronounced definitively, drinking up the last of his tea, and reaching for another bun. "'ere," he said suddenly, jerking up at me and giving me a penetrating look, "don't you go finkin' about goin' to that there Romford Market!," as if I'd been secretly planning all the while to go there in order to catch a rare Asian disease. "No, you stay away, boy," Mum hurriedly concurred, doubtless suddenly imagining me languishing on my bed upstairs. Then they all drank another cup of tea.

I would think of Cousin Albert upstairs in his bed somewhere in Rush Green, ruing the day he ever visited the Romford Market. "I just wanted to get some new trousers for work," he would murmur to himself, "an' I caught this bloody rare Asian disease! Last time I'm ever goin' there!" Aunt Ruby, who I had never seen either, would be there, nodding sadly. I imagined those trousers, cause of such distress, hanging limply in his cupboard, scorned by anyone who looked at them. I imagined Aunt Ruby as ruby red, and very big—maybe she was a "Great-Aunt"—running up and down the dark stairs of her council house day in day out bringing Albert plates of food and cups of tea and feeding him because he couldn't use his arms anymore. I could see the doctor paying a call once every few weeks, then slowly coming down the stairs, and talking with Aunt Ruby in a professional whisper while he put away his stethoscope in his black bag with a smart click of the clasp. "Not looking good, I'm afraid. Trouble is, this is a *very* rare Asian disease, and we don't know much about it. I hear there's a fresh outbreak of it in Malaya. Maybe we'll learn something there. I'll call in again in a couple of weeks. Chin up."

It usually took some time for Albert's condition to be dissected in satisfying detail: loss of the use of his arms, his legs, when exactly he would go blind and deaf and what this would mean for poor Ruby, who had plenty on her plate, what with having to change his bedpan all the time, since he was losing control down there as well. But eventually it would dwindle to an end, and then their collective attention turned to me. "'ow's the boy doin', then?" someone would venture, and so the process would begin. "Well, I tried to get 'im apprenticed to the butcher's down on Broad Street, but nothin' came of that." "Nah, can't see 'im doin' that. No good, eh, boy?" (said with a look at me that was at once conspiratorial and evaluative). "'ow's school, goin' then?" "'e's got the Eleven Plus comin' up," Mum replied before I could say anything. "Your Pauline did a treat with that, eh, got 'er O levels now, too," a mysterious cousin chipped in. "Clever girl, that un, she'll get on," someone else said. (I looked into the fire, seeing all sorts of figures from my comic books leaping there.) "So wot you wanna do, boy?" My answer would vary from season to season: "Train driver," "Dressmaker," "Pastry Chef." The answer that stirred most enthusiasm was the first one. "Chip off the 'ol block," an uncle would say, smiling, and digging Granddad in the ribs. Granddad would look doubtful, since his grandson was hardly a chip off *his* ol' block so far as he could see. "'e's got your 'ands, girl," the musty relation would say to Mum. "An' 'e's got 'is Dad's 'air," another would add. "'ose *nose* d'ya think 'e's got, then?" an aunt would inquire. After a while, Mum would release me, so I could go play outside. "Don't go too far," she'd say. And Granddad thundered as I was leaving the room, "An' don't go finkin' 'bout goin' to that bloody Romford Market!"

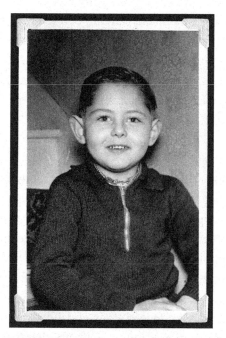

Kevin sitting on staircase in Rowdowns Road

Before getting on my bike and going to knock on Eddie's front door, I'd go upstairs to the carsey, and have a look at myself in the mirror. I had Mum's hands, Dad's hair, and every last bit of me had been assigned to someone or other in the family, going back to the Doomsday Book that the photograph album sometimes seemed to be on those occasions. Yet I couldn't see any of it myself. Maybe they were all wrong. Maybe it was all a huge pretense, since grown-ups couldn't be trusted anyway; maybe they were given the wrong baby at the hospital! Then I remembered I had been born at home, when Mum and Dad were living in South Ockendon. My bright idea deflated like a balloon that had got a hole when tying it up at the bottom. I looked and tried to see my Mum's or Dad's face in mine, but saw nothing of the sort, and imagined the day when one or the other would begin to appear. I would be thirty, living in a flat above a shop in Seven Kings or Rainham, shaving before going to work, and then would suddenly see that I was slowly becoming my father or a male version of my mother. But it all seemed improbable, and there was still time to spend some time at Parsloes Park with Kevin and Eddie, or even get up to Eastbrookend if we were quick about it.

———▼———

People often say that they had happy childhoods, and I've often wondered what they mean, and have asked myself if my childhood was a happy one. I lived a divided life, unhappy at school and hugely relieved when out of it, and yet I was insulated from school and home alike by layers and layers of milky emotions I couldn't name. I would have to chisel my way through time, I knew, but maybe I could do so by being to the side of things, being the one who just tagged along and didn't say much.

I was mostly contented at home, luxuriating in the warmth of Mum's sewing business, though from time to time my parents' frustration with my weak showing at school—not knowing the times table, and not even knowing how to tell the time—flared into anger with me or, rather, perhaps, at who I would become. They must have seen a version of the man I would become who appeared to me at the butcher's, but perhaps more feckless because of not having had an apprenticeship. For me, the apparition was more appealing. I would be free of school and also, when my parents became inarticulate with anger, free of them as well. The mystery of adulthood would finally be mine, and the heart of that mystery was freedom to do just what you wanted in your time off. I would be one of those silent men you saw in the Fanshawe Tavern or the Church Elm sitting alone, reading the evening paper, and having a beer after work. Then I'd heat up a Fray Bentos pie or Vesta Curry up in my flat, read the paper for a bit, maybe watch the telly, have a Lyons Individual Fruit Pie every now and then, and go to bed. At least I would have a warm bed and enough heat in the flat. Maybe one day I'd meet a nice girl from one of the local shops or at the Fanshawe and we'd settle down somewhere. For the life of me, I couldn't see what was so very wrong with this picture. It fitted most of the grown-ups I knew. Even better, I would return to the fantasy of life with Dominique in Rennes. I would be in my pastry shop there, saying *Bonjour, Madame!* And when I would get home Dominique would call me *chéri*, and there'd be more French kisses.

One day, after one of my parents' moments of exasperation at their image of my future, it struck me that I didn't need to wait to realize this modest dream. I would run away! While they were all comatose before the paraffin and the telly, I went up to my bedroom and rummaged around to find a suitcase. Under my bed there were lots of things, and I pulled them out. There were my sister's dolls; they looked at me with their blank, cold eyes. I found a little cardboard suitcase, and threw a few things into it—some socks, underpants, a shirt, a couple of comics— and then, very quietly, slipped out the front door. It was winter, and already dark; the bleak wind on my face gave an edge to my newfound freedom. My future was rushing towards me! I crept down Rowdowns Road, past the hated school, and made my way to Gorsebrook Park. It was deserted, and the trees and bushes looked eerie at night. I wandered around for a while, too apprehensive to walk down the avenue with tall dark trees on either side, and then two things slowly dawned on me: I hadn't got any food, and couldn't think of anywhere to go. I had needed a plan and some money to get away, perhaps down to Cornwell or up to Scotland where no one would know me. So I abruptly went home, with the intention of saving up my pocket money to make the big escape, and set up a new life in St. Ives, where someone at school had gone on holiday and who beamed about it, or Inverness, which sounded like a faraway place I'd read about in a comic and so far away no one would ever be able to find me. Then, after a while, I would go to Rennes and life would be good. (I knew exactly where it was, having looked it up in my school atlas.)

I reached the house, and expected my parents to have discovered my absence and to be lamenting their harshness to me. How they would welcome me back, and vow to be better parents! I opened the door, which was never locked until my parents went up to bed, and crept in. Mum, Dad, and Pauline were sitting in exactly the same place, transfixed by a show on the TV, and didn't see me coming in. No one had even noticed I wasn't in the house! I climbed the stairs in the dark to my bedroom, at once angry and relieved to be home and warm, fell asleep, and for the next couple of weeks stored up my pocket money before one Saturday morning I spent it all on comics at the Broad Street Market.

3 ▸

That overcast day I walked the little way to school to take the Eleven Plus with the feeling that the future had finally got me cornered. My long days of wandering the streets and parks had contracted to a corridor I had to walk down, a room I had to enter, and a chair I had to sit on.

The Eleven Plus was completely unlike any of the tatty exam papers that Fergie had passed out to us in the preceding months. I opened the booklet that smelled of ink and glue, my heart beating madly in my ear, and found the instructions unintelligible. The problems bore no resemblance to any that I had ever seen before. Within the first few minutes, I knew that I would fail. My beating heart told me so. The examination started with questions about arithmetic, and I spent far too much time writing the nine times table on the examination paper, working it out first on my fingers. I knew what the whole ordeal meant: I would have to go to Goresbrook Road School, which had a terrible reputation for gangs and bullying. One of those bigger Goresbrook boys was once seen in our school playground with a gun, and we knew what some of them could do. (One lad the year ahead of me had been grabbed by a couple of Goresbrook boys in winter and made to stick his tongue on a frozen pipe.) We were kept inside that day, and the police even visited the school and poked around for a while to see if the offender could be identified. I'd run into boys from Goresbrook on the weekend when larking about in the streets around home with a dustbin lid for a shield and a plastic sword in hand; they cruised around in twos and threes on racing bikes, checking out the local parks for opportunities to make trouble. It was always smart to be home before dark. Once I wasn't, and a big one in drainpipes stopped me at the corner of Rowdowns Road and Downing Road and, showing me his flick knife, said he wanted me to take down my pants. I'd been in our school toilets, seen what was scrawled over the urinal, and had a vague idea what he was after. I ran for dear life.

I waited for the official letter to come about the Eleven Plus result, and one summer's day it arrived. My parents were out, and since the envelope wasn't glued down I could open it and read it. It was just like the examination, I couldn't understand a word of it. Yet my parents glumly told me my fate that evening: I'd be going to Goresbrook, or maybe somewhere else if they could arrange it, though that would be very difficult for them to do and they might not succeed. They didn't need much imagination to conceive of what would happen to me there. Nor did I. In the end, they managed to get me into Eastbrook Boys School, which I hadn't heard of and which was supposed to be a notch or two better. I had to take two Red Line buses to get there, the first one leaving from the Heathway, a few streets away. In the smog of an early winter's morning it was impossible to see the buses coming up the street; there would be a dull yellow glare, and suddenly a bus would materialize. I had to look hard to make sure it was the right number, and had to keep looking as we drove along to make sure I got out at the right stop in order to change buses. It was a tough school. At the start of the first day, there was a parade out in the winter air, new boys at the front, and a short, frail old teacher, wrapped up in a scarf, holding a curved ribbed cane that seemed almost as tall as he was, spoke to us. He picked out a new boy: "You there, Donnelly! Yes, *you!* Oh, *I* know *you,* my boy! I've caned your *father,* both your *uncles,* your two older *brothers,* and before long I'll be caning *you!*" The other teachers laughed.

The first day I made friends with a boy almost as scared as I was. We gravitated to one another, being opposites in some ways. He was handsome and had a very neat haircut; there were sores at the end of my lips, my ears stuck out; and my mother cut my hair to save a bit of money, and she was often in a rush when she did it. "Sit next to ya at lunch?" he asked. "Smashin'," I said. It was my first experience of institutional food, and truth to tell it was more plentiful and better than what I usually had at home. For a start, there was bread and butter pudding with sweet thick custard steaming over it, after a hot main course of something brown and salty. We never had "afters" at home unless it was a special occasion, and then it was usually creamed rice. We were the epitome of working-class post-War austerity, as I came to see long after, with ration books still present to the mind if not the hand. The classes were grim, barely able to be controlled. One new teacher was corralled near the blackboard; boys pushed their desks around him, and he had to stand there, defeated, until authoritative footsteps were heard coming down the corridor. Then the desks were smartly scraped back into place. Some kids smelled bad; nothing was taught, apart from maybe the virtue of sitting up straight and looking up; and caning was quick and common. Years later when I read Dickens's *Hard Times*, I realized that the decades had merely rung changes on a theme and hadn't altered it very much at all.

We walked from class to class, which was something new, and in those first few weeks we were more tested than taught. One roneo-ed multiple-choice test had the answers already filled in. "Don't copy those answers," the teacher said in an oily tone; "they were given by a boy who got half of 'em wrong." The questions made no sense to me, and fifty percent was better than what I usually got in tests. I checked the boxes according to the logic that a fair sprinkling of (a), (b), (c) and (d) answers would get me through. The test was never returned. One boy, who hailed from India, regularly asked teachers when we would be getting homework. His father was concerned about it. (Just hearing the word "homework" made me feel sick. There was nowhere to do it at home, and I'd get it all wrong in any case.) "A train has to be led to its tracks," the mathematics teacher, who was Indian, said reflectively. "But, at the moment"—he paused—"we are a long way from the tracks." He gave us addition problems with decimals on the blackboard to figure out, but if I had been taught decimals at Thomas Arnold I must have been dreaming at the time, since I had no idea what to do with them. How could numbers have a dot in them? We had to swap papers for the problems to be corrected, and mine were all wrong with several dots in each answer; but the teacher didn't collect the papers or record any marks. At least Mum and Dad wouldn't know. On the times one or the other would ask me how school was going, I would say I felt completely lost. "Just do yer best," Mum said, in her usual resigned tone.

The worst period was PE. It was even worse than Sport where we ran around the field early in the morning when the fog was still heavy and played a truncated version of rugby. Out of the fog a muddy ball would sometimes come flying my way, but I dithered and didn't know what to do with it, which meant that a bunch of boys fell on me and got the ball. But at least there was the fog to retreat into until I got my breath again. Not so with PE. Big, hairy, muscular, and expansively Welsh, the teacher also had a sadistic streak. He had us vaulting horses, climbing ropes, and jumping on a trampoline, none of which I could even begin to do; and so, inevitably, he made an exhibition of my ineptitude. ("Okay, boyos, have a rest and then let's see if Hart can climb up half a foot of rope!") I had a very bad run of Welsh teachers: two out of two were shockers, nothing at all like Jones the Steam. Then again, I had nothing at all to recommend me. I was jeered in the brisk showers after PE; no one wanted to know me.

My new friend never seemed to be around, and nowadays he sat elsewhere at lunch.

——— ▼ ———

I clearly had to find a way out of doing PE, but that was not going to be easy. I had used up my entire line of sickness credit while at Thomas Arnold. I managed once or twice to get a note from Mum to let me off because I had a stomachache, was getting a sore throat, or something of the sort. She didn't like to do it, having, like my father, a deep-seated fear of institutional authority. Perhaps the Headmaster of *that* school would come by as well, and then where would we be? The neighbors would talk! Maybe the family would be reported to that mysterious group "The Authorities" and that might muck up our application to go to Australia. Once again, their specter rose up before me. Those people ran the world: they were men with gray hair and glasses; they wore dark suits; had gone to "public schools," whatever they were; and had "gone up" to Oxford and Cambridge, each of which I understood to be like the Emerald City; and they were driven around London in shiny black cars. They were MPs, Lawyers, Clergy, Bankers, Doctors, Headmasters, Judges, Station Masters, and Policemen, even Gardeners. (My parents were scared stiff of walking on the grass in Hyde Park when vainly trying to find the statue of Peter Pan.) If they were politicians, they were called "Conservatives" or "Tories" ("bleedin' Tories," my grandfather would say). Harold Macmillan was one of them, but there were a great many others, I was told.

Having a note to be excused PE safe and sound in my pocket meant that I could stay in a warm classroom and do—nothing. I watched snow fall: the raw sky was beginning to flake. There were no books to read in the school, or none that I ever found. I never entered or even saw a library there. One time I showed my homeroom teacher a note, and he said that I would need to give it to the Headmaster. This was a new development, and I had a bad feeling about it. I dragged myself all the way to the end of the cold corridor, and found there, waiting there in the dark, four or five boys all huddled together. They had all been sent by teachers to get the cane. Usually the Deputy Headmaster did that, but he must have been away that day. I stood in line behind them, but they were in no hurry to go into the Headmaster's room, since they knew all too well what was waiting for them there. So they let the shadows cover them lest a teacher should see them and usher them in. Maybe enough hours would glide by and they would be forgotten. One of the bigger boys said that I should go in first; I would have preferred to wait in the grim dark for more of PE to slide into the past, but that possibility had straightaway withered after seeing those boys in the heavy shadows.

I had been in the same situation at Thomas Arnold two years before. I was sent to the office towards the end of the last week of school with a note to give to Fergie. There was to be a Christmas party the following afternoon, and all the parents had donated cakes and biscuits and drinks. All the kids were looking forward to it, including, I dare say, the three boys waiting desultorily outside the door. One was picking his nose and inspecting what he had found there. We'd all been fantasizing about the cakes for two or three days before school and at lunchtime. "My Mum's givin' a Battenberg cake!" someone would say. "I'll 'ave a slice of that!" would come as an excited response. "Mine's givin' a big plate of cheesecakes!" "I'll 'ave one of 'em, too!"

"Wot's your note say?" one boy asked another. "Says four. 'Ow about you?" "Says two." "Lucky ol' you." "You 'ere for cuts, too?" the third boy asked, looking at the note in my hand. I shook my head, and knocked on the door. A prune-faced old female teacher with wispy hair going everywhere at once opened the door, and I could see several other teachers were in the well-heated room with Christmas decorations all over. They seemed to be in a good mood. There, in the middle of the room, was a big table, with cakes and biscuits all spread out. "Please, Miss, I was told to give this to Mr. Ferguson." My eyes settled on the table. "He's just there," she said. Indeed he was, deep in a large armchair, with a substantial slice of fruitcake and a cup of tea on a side table. My shock at the spread on the table, and that it was being sampled ahead of the party, must have been apparent, since he laughed a little uneasily as he took the note. "Don't worry, boy, there'll be enough for you tomorrow," he said. "Just keeping our strength up." (A nearby teacher laughed.) I saw his cane leaning against his armchair.

I knocked on the Headmaster's door, and heard a voice reply, "Come!" I entered. The room was overheated and full of furniture smelling vastly of wood polish. The Headmaster at Eastbrook had gray hair, half-moon glasses, sported a limp gray moustache, and was seated behind a large dark brown desk; he wore a white shirt, tie, faun-colored V-neck pullover, and a brown tweed jacket. He looked weary, though this was just the start of the day. Was this Harold Macmillan? He was the spitting image of him, and he sounded as I imagined an Authority would sound. I knew that Macmillan was no longer Prime Minister; perhaps he had landed a job at Eastbrook. He got up and took a long, swishy rattan cane with a crook handle from his desk. "Come for the cane, have we?" he asked, looking over his glasses and straight into my soul. "Let's see the note, then." The blood must have drained from my face. "No-o-o, sir," I blurted out. "I have a note from my mother about PE!" Deflated, he scanned the note, and said, "Report to gym. Only light exercise! And send the next boy in." I got out, without delay, pointing the nearest boy to his fate, and dawdled back down the corridor, waiting at chilly corners for as long as I possibly could, and got to the class within minutes of it finishing. The PE teacher cast a dirty look in my direction. "Jones the Shit," I said to myself, but so deep

inside that it would have taken an hour to reach my lips or my
eyes.

———— ▾ ————

Lunchtime was the most dangerous time of day, since it was
when some of the school toughs went around trying to fleece
the younger boys for money or anything else we had on us. They
would march around in twos or threes and would surround
you, press you against a wall, or drag you into an empty corridor or the toilet block, rough you up a bit, and then take whatever they could find, adding a few punches in the bread box and
sometimes a couple of spits in the face for good measure. There
was nowhere in the playground that was safe, and it was strictly
forbidden to leave the school. I suppose that there was a clear
arrangement to keep the boys within the schoolyard so that they
didn't bother the girls in their school. We could see the girls
but that was as far as it went. A teacher would be stationed at
the gate. Likewise, bullyboys lounged outside the dining room,
waiting for the small fry to finish our pudding and custard and
venture out. We used to drag out our lunches for as long as we
could, but younger teachers were there to hurry us out in the
grainy, bitter life outside.

Another boy and I hit upon a plan to stay safe that was so simple that it came as a huge surprise that it worked. We would wait
for two or three boys to leave the dining hall together and then,
just as they were going through the door, make a dash for it. The
toughs being occupied with their fresh meat, we would stride
smartly down the corridor in the other direction. It worked!
We got outside the building, slipped through a gap between two
fences, where there was no teacher in sight, and ran towards the
Chase, a stretch of low open land with a pond, about eight or
ten minutes away if we went fast. To leave the school at lunch
time was strictly forbidden, and the Chase was absolutely out

of bounds. It was a wonder that I summoned the courage to go there most days of the week, and a greater wonder that I was never caught. I dread to think what would have happened. Even worse, what would have happened if we had run into some of the bullyboys who had had the same idea years before? We couldn't have been the only ones who had ever ventured to leave. Nor were we: two or three times we saw older boys in the distance, smoking and doing who knows what else. We kept our distance.

We would usually have no more than twenty minutes there, and the time had two dimensions that intersected perfectly: exhilaration and anxiety, on the one hand, and otherworldly tranquility, on the other. Slap bang in the middle of down-at-heel, working-class Dagenham, we were in a wetland, as though miles and miles out of London, somewhere near fields with bluebells and cows, where I imagined that the Green Bus Line would end. I would stand most of the time under a tree in green-ish light and watch mallards and shovelers gliding on the water, chuck stones into the pond, find a blotch of frogspawn and stir it around with a stick, or imagine the strange lives of fish down in the murky depths. We only ever got just inside the Chase on those lunchtimes, but it was at once hot adventure and safety for all of twenty minutes. We hastened back, getting close to the main gate just as the bell was ringing and the teacher vanishing inside the school; and since no one had missed us, no one was looking for us. There was something blessed in being so ordinary and so insignificant that you were not known by anyone, boy or teacher.

— ▼ —

The Chase was huge, and as it happened I had known it for years, though not the part closest to Eastbrook, and I hadn't the faintest idea there was a school nearby. On Saturday or Sunday, when still at Thomas Arnold, Kevin, Eddie, and I would go on our bikes to another open tract of council land known as Eastbrookend or—to Eddie, Kevin, and me—as Eastbrookland, which was next door to it, rougher than it, and inexhaustible. During the endless summer we haunted the place, or maybe it haunted us. We'd have as big a breakfast as we could manage, pack sandwiches in brown paper bags—usually made with Skippam's fish paste or cheese spread and uneven slices of limp tomato—a couple of hardboiled eggs, if there were any eggs in the house, a plastic water bottle filled right to the brim, and if we were lucky a Jaffa orange, and be off and away until just before dinner in the evening.

In those days Eastbrookland was mostly gravelly wasteland and wetland with some farmland fenced off in a half-hearted way. It was empty, apart from occasional tangles of skinheads wandering around and looking for trouble; but they weren't really interested in the likes of us. Once or twice I would see one of them with a crossbow or a homemade longbow; he was trying to shoot birds. The place was full of birds: I had never heard so many different calls. Or maybe he was aiming for one of those foxes you would sometimes catch a glimpse of, chestnut brown, like a conker. Any skinhead there would have a flick knife and an ex-army knife, bought cheaply down at Broad Street or over at Romford Market or Barking, which he would use to torture and kill anything he'd wing or wound. Every once in a long while, far in the distance, there would be a little knot of Bobbies staring at the ground; I suppose skinheads sometimes killed a farm animal and the farmer dialed 999. This wasteland would be just the place to chuck a body, Eddie, Kevin, and I agreed, and once we dared each other to open the door of a big fridge, dumped along with other rubbish, which had lost its handle, and seemed a likely place for a corpse to have been left and missed by the police. It had a black swastika sprayed on it, after all. There was nothing inside, only a sick stale smell, and yet the year before a smaller boy had got himself locked into an abandoned fridge just like that not far from where we used to play, and his body was found a few days later. The story got around the school, and we all thought that a skinhead had pushed the kid in and left him there.

There were huge piles of rubbish, little mountains of sand and gravel, ruined mattresses with springs sticking out, babels of rubble dumped there from the Blitz, thick tufts of long grass and dandelions, thistles and nettles aplenty, rotting cardboard boxes that had been left out in the rain, and tracks that seemed to go on and on and lead nowhere at all. Or if they did, it was only to a lake that had filled an old pit, or a group of bushes that none of us had seen before. London stepped back, and there appeared a sky more immense than I had ever seen. We'd leave our bikes near a stream, and then wobble over an exposed log, jump to the other shore, or, if defeated by distance or fear of slipping, wade through it and head off for parts unknown with brown water sloshing in our socks and shoes. It was easy to fantasize about being in another country or in another age, though we seldom let our minds stray far away from England. I grew up on stories of the Blitz, of my nan, mother and neighbors taking shelter in the tube, and this was the closest I would ever get to those buildings blown up in the middle of the night. We would look for German bombs, and were always disappointed, but one day we found some old cartridges, probably left over from someone doing some target practice; they were glacial in the hand, and made my heart thump. "I wanted to kill someone," the one I was holding said to me. I took it home and hid it underneath my bed in one of the boxes where Pauline kept her old dolls. (They looked at me again with their cold, fixed eyes.) I wished I'd got the knuckleduster that Kevin found one day beneath a tree and used to try on when round his house. We'd pretend to be escaping after being part of the Great Train Robbery, or having derailed a train by putting a big stone on the tracks, or being back in the age of the dinosaurs and being tracked by a t-rex. Or we'd play or half-play at getting lost; and it was easy to get dehydrated, since we never seemed to take enough water with us on the warm days and never wore hats. On those days it was good to come across a blackberry bramble.

I often wanted to look for bird eggs, which I had been collecting for a couple of years and which were plentiful when I was out and about in March and April, more so than in summer. The best place for bird nesting was Sussex, where we would stay for a weekend with Aunt Lucy and her husband, who were better off than us, and where my parents kept looking adrift, not knowing which knife to use at meals and sitting awkwardly at tea time, not knowing where to put their hands or what to say. I'd get out into the country, walk up lanes and climb over fences, looking here, there, and everywhere, taking in the smell of wet earth and rotting leaves. Sometimes, after rain, I'd be able to smell out a damp nest. Mostly, though, I had to ply my hobby in the East End, where the pickings were far slimmer.

I was not much of a tree climber, yet I managed to shin myself up a few feet when a nest was within view, taking one or two warm robin or chaffinch eggs in my hand, and trying to keep them safe all day. I loved the light blue of the robin eggs, the pink splotches on the chaffinch eggs, and their wonderful fragility. In some corner of my mind I imagined that I had been mysteriously charged to discover those tight little cups made of sticks and moss and spider's web in which they incubated their eggs and to bring their treasure safely home. Sometimes there were dead eggs that hadn't been tossed out of the nest, and I took them. But I preferred by far to feel the warmth of living eggs in my palm.

I probably conceived this boyish Quest-Romance when reading one of the comic books Mum had got for me in the local newsagent. I had a steady diet of them, especially *The Beano* and

The Eagle. When I got home, Mum would stand at the front door, delicately pierce each egg with a pin, and blow the yolk out; and then I would add them to my collection, which was housed in an old picnic basket. Sometimes my mother would sigh when I brought home an egg, or if she found a dead embryo, but she never said I should stop. My parents thought I was just taking an interest in nature, which was a good thing as far as they were concerned. Better to be at Eastbrookend giving grief to birds than hanging round the streets picking up bright ideas from rockers and borstal boys. But I wasn't much of a candidate to end up like Reggie and Ronald Kray.

Inevitably, we really did get lost sometimes, and we exhausted ourselves running around trying to remember a particular tree or look of a path that would get us back to where we had left our bikes. There was always a fear that we'd find them, late in the afternoon, with a bunch of skinheads sitting around them, smoking and waiting for us to turn up, but that never happened. (We'd heard stories that one skinhead would grab you, drag you down, and pin your hands behind your back and another would hold open your mouth, while a third would piss down your throat.) The languid afternoons seemed to stretch out forever, especially one Saturday, just before the Eleven Plus, when I noticed that it was getting dark but my watch—the first I'd had, bought at the Broad Street Market, a reward for learning how to tell the time— said steadily that it was only two o'clock. We trusted my watch, which was the only one we had, until we saw the sun glowering low through the gathering clouds, which threatened rain. As darkness came, we couldn't find our way back to our bikes; we crashed through bushes, scratched our arms and faces, ran this way and that. I passed a small lake, surrounded by reeds, with swans calmly paddling on its water beneath a purple sky, and vowed that I would return to that enchanted place. Eventually, we got on those frail bikes and pedaled home as fast as we

could, along streets with cars with their headlights glaring down
Dagenham Road and Rainham Road. My parents were frantic
with worry; my father walloped me good and hard and only later
saw that the two bob watch they had bought me was broken. Try
as I might, I could never again find that lake with the swans. I
told myself that you had to be lost to get there.

———▼———

Every year my parents put money in a rusty blue tin box with a
picture of the Queen and Prince Philip that they hid on the top
shelf of the pantry so that we could have a two-week holiday in
August. We always stayed in a caravan park, and it was usually
at Folkestone, near the Channel, in Kent. The countdown for
the departure day started early for me; I'd cross off days in the
calendar hanging in the kitchen as soon as I got up. I'd look at
the rows of X's and they were immensely comforting. The end
is coming! It probably started early for my parents as well: they
had to book a caravan and hire a driver to take us down the coast,
and those were doubtless their biggest expenses for the year. As
the holidays drew near, we would talk at school about where we
would be going. "Southend," Ronnie would say, a little glumly.
"Me, too," Paul would add, sniffling (he always had a cold), "as
usual." Bournemouth was another place some families went, so
were Brighton and Clacton. Others would go to visit relations in
unknown places like Luton or Colchester. But I would say "Folkestone." "Lucky ol' you" (said flatly), I'd hear, since Folkestone
wasn't regarded as one of the *better* places for a holiday; it had
little sand and many pebbles on the beach, but I liked those peb-
bles and regretted when we had to go to Southend when money
was scarce.

We'd get a bus to Southend and stay for just a few days. Mum,
Dad, and Pauline would rent deck chairs and sit for hours on the
beach, sunning their white, flabby bodies in the weak sunlight,

Mum and Dad and caravan

leaving me free to roam around the pier and the shops, looking at the lurid postcards, all bums and tits, sometimes buying a stick of rock with my pocket money (pink on the outside with *Southend* written in pink all down the white center) and taking in the salt air. We'd take sandwiches to eat on the beach, and no matter how firmly they were wrapped in greaseproof paper they invariably got sand in them. "Wot's for lunch, then?" Dad would ask. "'am, cheese and sand," Mum would answer despondently. Fed up with such fare, we'd go in search of a cheap dinner after a night or two down there. Once we found a little place called The Hole in the Wall, and in truth it was just that. It looked spooky from the outside, like the entrance to a ghost train ride at the fair. So Dad went in ahead of us, and was soon lost in dark. He called to us to come in, and it turned out to be a dance hall; but you could get something to eat there if you were quick about it.

We sat down at a rickety Formica table by a wall, and in the

half-light ordered pies, chips, and tea; there was a smell of cigarettes and stale beer. A band started to set up for later that evening. A fat man with a dark suit tied round his gut with a single
button was in charge, making sure that the place was properly
tarted up with glittering lights and loops of tinsel; and then
a younger man, also in a black suit, with a black pompadour,
started to assemble a drum kit. After a while, Mum remarked on
another family on the other side of the hall. They were Indian.
"Wonder wot they make of Southend?" she said, half to herself
and half to Dad, "s'pose they don't 'ave beaches an' piers an' slot
machines where they come from." Then she added, "Fancy traveling 'alfway round the world to get 'ere, an' leavin' everythin'
behind." They had a boy about my age, and he made a beeline
for the drummer, asking him about his set, how long it took to
set up, how it was packed away, what the hide was on the drums,
how the snare worked, and lots of other questions. My mother's attitude changed to appreciation. "'e'll get on!" she nodded
approvingly to Dad. Then a cloud of irritation passed over her
face. "Ain't there anythin' *you* wanna ask 'im?" she asked me,
impatiently. There wasn't, I just wanted the pie and chips. She
looked pointedly away.

It was dark when we left The Hole in the Wall, and as we
made our way back to the outside through the black tunnel,
hands touching the wall, there were teenagers pushing past us
for the dance. Cheap music started to envelop me. I could smell
the girls' perfume as I walked behind Dad, and I started to walk
more slowly. "C'mon, son, we gotta get 'ome," he said when I
fell a few feet behind. We had to cross a park to get back to the
dingy little hotel where we were staying. A few feet inside, a girl
of about eighteen ran past us, crying her heart out, and quickly
vanished in the dark. The whole park was suddenly thick with
raw emotion. "Wonder wot's up with 'er?" Dad said. "Dunno,"
Mum replied. "Some boy, I s'pose." I thought of the girl running

ahead of us, hair flying, sobbing. Where was she going? Would this be the worst night of her life? Is this the sort of thing that life holds in store? Then Dad broke wind. Pauline leaned over to me, and whispered, *"Der Vater."* I must have looked puzzled. "It's German for 'father,'" she said.

Most years, though, we went to Folkestone, and that was always for two weeks. One morning, bright and early, a clean black car would pull up smoothly outside our front door and sit there humming quietly to itself. We'd fill it with our plump suitcases, Dad would run inside and turn off the gas, and then we'd be off. We dressed up for the occasion, and I'd feel overly scrubbed and combed as I sat in the back seat. What with all the twists and turns, and the lack of fresh air, I would always get car-sick, requiring the driver to stop two or three times so I could throw up into a paper bag. He'd get a little grumpy because he had to be home for tea, and Mum would sometimes get irritated. "You're just doin' it to show me up!" We'd arrive in good time. Just one more turn of the road and I'll see the sea, I'd tell myself over and over as the time went by—*see the sea, sea the sea, see the see,* and so on—after we had passed Maidstone or Ashford, and I was always far too early, and had to say it two dozen times or more before the Channel came into view. Just think: France was right over the water!

I loved it there: the caravan ("cheap and cheerful," Mum would say), the bushes near the park that beckoned as soon as I had unpacked, the pebbly beach, and of course the salty taste of the sea air. Only once or twice did I ever brave going into the water—it was usually too frigid to do so, for a start—but I made sandcastles by collecting sand wherever I found it and bring-ing it back in a pail, and decorated them with shells and peb-bles; played cricket with Dad (sporting a knotted handkerchief on his head) on grass near the beach; mooched around the sea front, looking at the boats and hanging around the amusement

Kevin on the beach

park; and walked around the streets of the town, peering into the gift shop windows. Had I saved up enough pocket money for the whole two weeks? Usually not: I'd run out and have to cadge money from Dad for ice creams. I'd usually join forces with a few boys, also down from London, to range around the streets and play war or cricket in the nearby fields. They would come and go, and when a new boy just got off the train and took his first whiff of sea air for the year he'd treat any boy who'd been there for a week or more as a towering authority on the town and all the thrills it tightly held behind its staid appearance. Differences would appear: one family would take their kids to a restaurant facing the beach for lunch, while the rest of us had to have sandwiches made in the caravans. (One boy staying in a tent mostly lived off condensed milk sandwiches, with a sugar sandwich once a week for a treat.) "Goody gumdrops," someone would say, sourly, when a boy came back from a restaurant to join us after lunch and told us about the sausages, eggs, and chips he'd had for lunch.

Mum and Dad would stock up with books of crossword puzzles for the holiday, to which Mum would always add what she called "a dirty book." That novel was always a magnet for my attention. One year it was a paperback copy of Harold Robbins's novel *The Carpetbaggers*, which I thought must have been a story about people stealing carpets. It had been banned, I had heard Mum say breathlessly, but now you could get it if you went up to London. Maybe Foyles had it, but the place was a rabbit warren and she didn't want to ask the man at the counter where it was. She certainly got it from somewhere or other, though; maybe through her old friend Kitty in Bethnal Green. Stealing carpets must be a very bad thing indeed! But what was the attraction? Carpet was everywhere. I would pick up the fat paperback when everyone was out of the caravan, but couldn't make head or tail of it. Hours stood still when the other boys were kept home or had gone home, and there was no cricket to play. I needed other things to do, especially as the evening drew on and drew away my friends who had to go home for dinner. Pauline gave me a ripe opportunity one year.

There was a boy she showed some interest in from day one of the holiday. He was young, slim, dark haired, but his distinguishing feature was that he always wore red socks over hush puppies. So I called him "Red Socks." I followed him around the caravan park and into the town with a little notebook I'd made from toilet paper for the express purpose of taking down details of his route, once with a chocolate pipe in my mouth. As I had no talent whatsoever as a private detective, he saw me following him almost from the beginning and, after a day or so of being tagged by a boy who hid, usually unsuccessfully, behind trees or caravans, he confronted me. "Hey there! Stay where you are. Now why are you following me?" he asked in a pleasant, educated

Pauline by caravan

voice, looking straight into my eyes. "My sister likes you!" I blurted out. "Is she the one with glasses in that yellow caravan over there?" he asked. I nodded. So they met and went to the pictures once or twice. It was an adventure for my sister as well as for me. I went back to looking in the bushes for nests, and already I could feel a shadow approach: the end of the holiday when we'd have to return to Rowdowns Road and, far worse, I'd have to go back to school. The days between Fergie and I were diminishing. The thought prowled round and round my mind. Once again, I'd be crossing off the days on the calendar, and the last two or three were almost unbearable. The caravan was brim full of excess time, the time that comes only when something is over and done with and one can't move on, knowing that moving on means going into the dark.

———▼———

One day, when back home, when Dad was still on his break from Beckton, he and Mum got up especially early and dressed up as though they were going to Buckingham Palace. I had never seen my father wear a tie in the morning, but he did on that day: it was thin and black, and I dare say that it was the one he wore on his wedding day years before and had put on only when going to "dos" after weddings for which Mum had made the dresses. Mum put on a dark pink twin set, made of Terylene, and wore what I thought was a string of pearls around her neck. She put on lipstick and perfume and took a long time with her hair. They were both nervous. They had to go to Barking to be interviewed by the Bank Manager there because they wanted to open an account. (I presume that this was in order to give them a better chance of being accepted as migrants to Australia. The quick and complete failure of their bid to move to Canada had thoroughly shaken them, and they knew that this was their only chance to leave England. A bank account would raise them an inch or two in the eyes of the world.)

"You got the wotsit, Rose?" She had: it was a small walnut box that Granddad had made and that I hadn't seen before. I suppose it contained banknotes that they had been putting aside apart from what went into the tin box. "Better keep it safe." It went into a large bag she was carrying. So they went off to Barking, and returned enormously relieved and very pleased with themselves; they'd even had something to eat in a café on the way home. They had been allowed to deposit some money in the local bank! That night they talked about the Bank Manager at dinner: he sat behind a dark brown desk, had gray hair and a black suit. He wrote with a black fountain pen with a gold nib, and spoke "all Bay Window." Mum did all the talking, because Dad always got tongue-tied on such occasions. "Now why do you need a bank account, Mr. Hart?" the Manager had evidently asked. "To save up, sir!" Mum quickly said, "to 'av a little on the side for a rainy day." And that must have been a reasonable answer, and probably the Manager was relieved that they didn't want a loan. Certainly having a bank account enabled them to fill in one of the forms that Australia House eventually sent to them. Maybe they had to show evidence of having at least forty pounds in the bank to cover the fee for migration.

⸻ ▼ ⸻

My parents never took me to church. The topic came up once or twice when my father thought I should go to Sunday School. The very word "school" frightened me anyway, and since I had never been to church the idea of going to school on Sunday, as well as on five days a week, scared me half to death with thoughts of dark pews and tests on all those incomprehensible names I had seen when glancing over pages of my father's inscrutable Bible: Baal-berith, Haahashtari, Melchizedek, and the island of Samothracia. I would surely fail, and there I would be with smelly old men, each looking like a pint of Guinness, probably talking in the dark about mystifying and embarrassing things, like Jesus's feet, and from time to time pointing to a slipper or flicking canes. I did all I could to get out of it, and it didn't take much effort, since my mother didn't fancy the idea one little bit. She was of the view that we find out about religion only when we die. My father had been defeated in a skirmish, I knew, and for a while the house had a frustrated air of *Should've* countered by *Let Orf.* The Church was an Authority too, but for some reason it could be sidestepped, or at least Mum thought it could. Over the next few days Dad looked gingerly around, as if Eternity were leaning down and frowning at him and me.

I used to think about Mum's view of the afterlife at night in bed before falling asleep. There would be a Great Judgment of some vast sort, with all of humanity in a massive church hall receding to infinity on all sides, and God would be sitting on an immense Throne up front, but impossible to see because of all the people much closer, rows and rows of all those dead men, women, and children who had lived in Athens and Rome and in the Middle Ages, right up to dead soldiers from the War. There would be a hum of incomprehensible foreign languages, and angels floating around shushing everyone. There would be higher ranking angels near God, too, tremendous numbers of them, all golden and with the solid bearing of statues, and saints as well, with haloes much like Saturn's rings over their heads, and most of them looking very cross at the vast unwashed crowd before them. Some angels up front would be holding enormous thick volumes, and you would hear every so often a name. "Rafferty, P., early nineteenth century, Dublin." And then there'd be a long litany of his sins, lots of them presumably relating to the mysterious "dirty secrets" that my mother often alluded to when gossiping with the neighbors about Christine Keeler and others like her. Government scandal lasted for a long time once it had reached the East End, like filthy water in a blocked drain. We would be standing for hours on end while the Judgment droned on and on. And then there would be solemn trumpets, and a long silence, followed by God finally thundering, "It was the *Methodists!*" (or the Catholics or the Presbyterians or the Jews or some other group that had a little church or synagogue in Barking, Ilford or Romford; the poor old Church of England never seriously appeared as a possibility). I imagined my mother at once satisfied to know the truth at last and very upset, wailing to God, in the stunned silence of all humanity, "But 'ow could I 'ave *known?*"

I went to churches often, though I almost never got inside

and never for a service. Mum, being a dressmaker specializing in brides, had lots of invitations to local churches for weddings. They were always on a Saturday. We would get to the church quite late, so as not to have to go in, and wait until the bride and groom came out, a little dizzy in the sudden sunlight and flash upon flash, and were showered with confetti. Mum would take a tradeswoman's interest in how the dresses appeared at the moment they would be recorded on film. Sometimes she was included in a group photograph with the bride and bridesmaids. ("Smile for the little birdie," said the photographer in the check jacket from the big studio in Barking.) She had grown close to the girls over the evenings spent with them and warmly wished them well. The bride would whisper something in Mum's ear. "Get away with ya," she'd say, smiling broadly. Sometimes she and my father were invited to the reception, and I stayed at home with Kim, who belonged body and soul to my mother (and who howled disconsolately and without respite when she was away); Charlie the mynah bird who hopped about in his cage and said, raucously, now and then, "Watch that pussycat!"; and the very cat he cautioned us to be aware of, Bobbie, who jumped on my bed, formed herself into a dark purring mound on my feet, and so kept me company in the dark hours when they were both away. I would sometimes hear the click of the front door around eleven o'clock or even midnight, hear Kim jump up at Mum, and then fall into a deeper sleep.

———— ▾ ————

Saturday afternoons at Nan and Granddad's were mostly the same, week in and week out. There would be the heavy lunch. ("Could've used Angie in the war," Dad would say to Mum on the long walk home down Hedgeman's Road, "'er pastry could've sunk the 'ole Gerry navy!") Then we'd watch the wrestling or boxing on TV, while Granddad sat in his armchair with his pipe and Mum smoked half a pack of cigarettes. There was a bit of talk over lunch, then silence, then a sprinkling of talk about work or relations, usually over two or three cups of stewed tea. Granddad always had the floor, and his talk revolved around three main topics of complaint against the world: the closure of the docks, a Jewish barber he had once patronized, and a Catholic woman who lived over the road in the banjo. The stories varied little week by week, but they rose and fell in intensity. "Ain't goin' no more to that bleedin' four by two barber," he'd say. "Ran into 'im t'other day over in Ilford: "Ere, 'ow come you ain't been round to 'ave your 'air cut?' he asked. I'll tell you why," Granddad said, warming to his story, "'cause you keep tryin' to sell me all that bleedin' 'air lotion and combs an' God knows wot else!'" (Pause.) "Can't trust 'em Jew boys, always bloody tryin' to sell yer somethin' or t'other."

On the other side of the banjo, and a few doors up, there was a middle-aged woman with red hair done up high and loose on her head. Her husband had left her a year or two back, and she had "gone to the dogs," it was firmly agreed by my grandparents and parents. She'd taken to drink, they said with a *tut* or two in their voices, and I was scared when, once or twice, she ran out to see me when I was playing in the banjo, and spoke rather wildly to me, in tears, about her son who had been taken by her husband. Once she embraced me with great feeling and told me to be a good man when I grew up. Another time she must have got in a bad way, and we could hear her crying on a Saturday afternoon. "I'm bloody well fed up with that there woman an' 'er palaver!" Granddad said, and marched out the front door. "Shuttup, will yer! That bawlin' won't bring 'im back!" he yelled. (I imagined neighbors cowering inside their houses, peering through their closed curtains.) Granddad certainly disapproved strongly of "drink," especially hard drink, and limited himself to a "quiet ale" every once in a while, usually when seeing his lieutenant from army days up in London. (For all his dislike of the establishment, he highly respected army officers. *They* weren't "lazy sods." Nor were the Queen and the Queen Mother. The same couldn't be said for "Phil the Greek," however. "Wot she wanna go an' marry *'im* for? Bloody foreigners!" One time Dad tried to explain that the Windsors had changed their name in the First World War from Saxe-Coburg and Gotha, and that they were originally German. "Nar, can't be, Jim," Granddad said, "we were at bloody war with 'em there Gerries."

The root of his distaste for the woman over the road, though, was that she was of Irish extraction and Catholic. "Bleedin' superstition!" he'd say, beginning his tirade. "Them bloody priests takin' money from 'em all the time when they can't afford nothin' anyways, an' tellin' 'em wot they can and can't do. And who knows wot they get up to in those bleedin' confessionals? Bet your last farthin' they got a bottle of somethin' in there. 'alf-drunk most of the time, mark my word. I saw enough of those buggers in the army. Lazy sods the lot of 'em!" He was firmly convinced that the redhead over the road had guns beneath her bed, like all Catholics, and that one day the Pope would rally them and they would try to take over the country. "Bleedin' Guy Fawkes all over again!" he said, shaking his head.

---- ▾ ----

"I'll take the boy up to London for the Tattoo!" So Granddad announced one Saturday afternoon at lunch. My parents seemed pleased, and so a date was set. He was very concerned that I would have to negotiate the tube, especially the escalators, and so he gave me lessons in his living room how to step onto and off of them. It was very important, he thought, to enter and leave an escalator with one's right foot. He showed me what he had in mind. "Now you 'avva try," he said. I did just as I was asked. "Love-er-ly!" he said. And so we could go. I was very apprehen-

Kevin and Pauline with dubious Santa

sive, since I had seen a tattoo once or twice, and I didn't want one at all. Perhaps all men had them, though I couldn't see one anywhere on Granddad or Dad; maybe they were hidden. When I had been put on Santa's knee once I saw that *he* had tattoos all down his arms. Perhaps you got them about my age, and it was never talked about. Dad and Granddad never wore short sleeves, and only rarely had their sleeves rolled up very far. I'd had a transfer or two from a Lucky Bag on my arm every now and then. What a mistake that had been! It must have given Granddad the idea I wanted a proper tattoo!

The scene swam before me: I would get off the tube, right foot first, and then be taken into a dingy little shop in an alley off one of the main roads, and a man covered in tattoos and smoking a fag would have me lay down, and then inscribe whatever Granddad wanted on my arm, leg, or maybe somewhere else. What would it be? Would I get a choice? I had better think of something. I revolved some possibilities: *Dominique* in a heart with an arrow going through it (but how to explain that to Pauline, Mum, and Dad?), *Pam* (with much the same decorations, and with similar difficulties), *Folkestone* (but what if I went to the beach at Brighton?), the Union Jack (probably the best all round, especially with Granddad there, but what if we really did move to Australia?) The prospect was scary beyond belief. But no one could contest anything Granddad said, except perhaps Nan when she got angry with him, and even that was risky—I certainly would never have tried it. There was that belt to think about. So I resigned myself to having something written on my arm, like the butcher at the Broad Street Market, that anyone could see when I wore a T-shirt in summer. I knew that it would hurt a lot, and presumably that was why I was going with Granddad: he wouldn't put up with any nonsense.

I came through my test of escalators in the tube with flying colors. Granddad was very pleased with me, and I thought to myself, "So I've passed the first test; I'll 'ave to try not to flinch when I get the tattoo." But we didn't go into a grimy little shop like the one I had imagined, and there was no man covered with tattoos. Instead, we stopped in another little shop and had cheese sandwiches with Branston pickle. "Like that, did ya?" he asked. I nodded. "Another satisfied customer!" he said, making his usual joke. Then we walked a few more blocks and entered a stadium and got a seat high up, towards the back. There was a long wait, and then soldiers in uniform came out and marched around this way and that; there was martial music, including bagpipes wailing, and a great deal of applause at certain sharp movements of the men, which made no sense to me at all. Granddad was loving every moment of it—I'd never seen him so happy—and all the time I kept thinking: after this, *I am being taken to get a tattoo.* But the afternoon wore on with much more of the same, and when we left, evening was already beginning to darken the streets. We went straight to the tube station and got on a train on the Upminster Line. No tattoo!

The next year Granddad had another idea. He would take me to Madame Tussaud's on Marylebone Road. I had no idea what it was, but when I got there I thought it would have suited Dad far more than Granddad who had never expressed the slightest interest in British history apart from the war, which was hardly history for him. By now I was completely fluent in the use of my right foot on the escalator; I put it out with the confidence of kings, for this was the way to my Granddad's heart. We waited and waited in the queue, and then the mass of people had to move on the double through the exhibit. There were Princesses Elizabeth and Margaret. "The spittin' image!" Granddad said, approvingly; it almost made up for him not being able to smoke his pipe in the exhibit. I had to push past people at times, especially in the Chamber of Horrors, to see the shadow of Jack the Ripper, lots of death masks, the guillotine, and—there he was again!—Guy Fawkes. But it was grand. Granddad was impressed by almost everything: his craftsman's appreciation of verisimilitude was in full blossom. He even liked the model kit you could buy of a Guillotine with a man strapped to it, though he didn't offer to buy me one. Mum might not have approved. (Nor, I thought, would Dominique.)

———▼———

I was mostly left to myself after school and the weekends: hours mucking about at one or another park, and entire days pretending to be soldiers or explorers or time travelers at East-brookland, mostly with Eddie and Kevin but sometimes, when they had to stay home, by myself: I lived deep within myself, and it took teachers and even my parents considerable effort to cross the distance from the outside world to my world. "'e's like a snail, that one," one relation said, "just pulls 'is head in." For my part, I came less and less to make that passage outside, and one consequence of that was that in my last year or so in London time started to dilate for me and sometimes to become unreal. At times I really was sick, usually just for a day or two, but sometimes for weeks at a time; and in those long periods I would lay in bed upstairs, mostly in a half-sleep, and the day would pass slowly over me. Once I slept through an entire day, and only decades later when I had children myself did I stop to wonder why neither parent checked on me. It was an outlier in a general pattern. Teachers preferred not to notice me, since communicating with me was so difficult. I was morbidly shy, frightened of adults, and shrank from their very presence. And my parents seemed resigned, most of the time, to the melancholy fact that their son lived at a tangent to normal life. A teacher had said once, "You'll have trouble with him one day when he breaks out of his shell." But that seemed improbable. "Maybe 'e'll snap out of it in time," Mum once said to Dad when I was in the kitchen.

Once I had novels about Doctor Dolittle to read, and library books about dinosaurs, I gave myself over to them when I was sick in bed and sufficiently well to read them; but even then I reverted to the practice of simply looking at the things in my room and concentrating on them until they started to step towards me. A lamp in a corner near the curtain would slowly move towards me away from the wall, yielding all its details in a minute or two. I could touch it and feel each bump of polish. Fever? Perhaps; but if so, there was something in the fever I was able to cultivate and reproduce. At other times I would glance at my life to come, that clerk living in a flat over a shop somewhere in the East End. One thing I thought was very likely: he would be going to church on Sundays, and going properly, not just standing outside. Lying in bed with a cold or a sore throat, all caused by being generally run down, I also pondered God. Bunyan had told me about God, and I had heard or read a little of the Bible, but beyond that I had had no religious education whatsoever. And yet I had the strongest conviction that God was real, and that he wasn't far away. Not that this was a comforting experience: what I had learned about God was that he was fire and smoke, and wanted boys to go to Sunday School, and that one had to climb a hill called Difficulty. Of course, I had absolutely no idea about Jesus, apart from the odd things that I had learned about him from hymns, which made no sense at all. The little I knew was that he had lived in Israel, somewhere near where Granddad served in the War, but in the hymns at school he was wandering around ancient Britain.

Only once did a C. of E. clergyman come into Thomas Arnold to teach us anything about God. Like swimming, it was not a common event. The clergyman was a very enthusiastic young man who took it upon himself to explain the Trinity. For once, I paid attention: here was a whole part of life that had been put to one side, covered over by silk, taffeta, tulle, and confetti. He explained that God is at once one and three. An impression was given of souls after death being like clouds with a human shape; we would all be singing praises to God; and we would all be gazing at him and only him. The first part seemed reasonable enough. The second was worrying, since it sounded just like morning hymns, and since I couldn't sing in tune, and couldn't tune a guitar, I imagined angels easily becoming exasperated with me. Did angels have canes? Chances are they would, I concluded. "How something can be one and three at the same time," the clergyman said, "is probably not clear to you." It certainly wasn't. He drew an equilateral triangle on the blackboard. "How many triangles are there on the board?" he asked, smiling. "One," a boy a couple of rows ahead of me volunteered. "Good, good," said the clergyman. "Now can someone else tell me how many sides it has?" "Three," said one of the girls. "Excellent!" said the clergyman, warming to his theological success. "It's exactly the same with God!"

I returned to this image many times over the months that followed, especially when I was ill in bed. I was dead, and therefore now made of something like fog, and heaven itself would be something like our playground on winter mornings. But morning hymns would last all the time, and we would always be facing an enormous equilateral triangle that we could make out every now and then. One of those sides was Jesus, but that made no sense at all, unless he was elongated very dramatically. He had been crucified, I knew, on a hill that didn't have a wall around it: were you stretched when that happened to you? I asked Dad, who I knew was quietly religious, but the most I got out of him was "Dunno" and a worried look. (Mum never liked talk about religion at home, or anywhere else, for that matter.) My mind wandered off to the more interesting question whether one could have girlfriends in heaven. Maybe there were dishy angels, and you could go out with them on days off from the endless choir practice. I'd try to get them to take off their wings for a while, so I could hold them tight. "God won't mind!" I'd say. Maybe you could go on day trips to other parts of heaven: the French sector attracted me a great deal. There would be buses, also made of something like cloud, so they would travel in a flash. But everyone had to stay in his sector, that seemed clear, and so I'd have to be back to get my own seat before the Eternal Triangle that saw everything.

A few years later, in year eight Religious Education at Oxley State High School, another young C. of E. clergyman took the classes. He started by telling us how long after Jesus's death the Gospels were written. "How could you remember anything about Jesus after all that time?" he asked. We agreed: it would be hard. Then he threw another question at us. "But who could possibly forget things like *that*?" We agreed again. Having shown his dialectical skills, he rushed headlong over a cliff to explain the mystery of the Trinity. Again, I paid close attention, thinking that if I was to spend all eternity with God I really should learn something about him. Once again there came the inevitable question how something could be at once one and three, but Anglican Theology had taken a huge step forward in the last couple of years, and this clergyman had another explanation. "Have you ever seen ice?" he asked. "And water?" Yes, we had seen that, too. "And steam?" Of course: when the kettle boiled. "Well, what are they?" he asked expansively and leaned back in his chair. After a few false tries, an answer came: H_2O. "Yes!" he exclaimed: three in one! It was hardly better than the most holy Equilateral Triangle, but I quietly felt a prick to find out more by myself, and promised my future self that by the time I was he I would have devoted myself to the question.

———— ▼ ————

I came home one afternoon after playing in Goresbrook Park to find my sister lying on the settee with her face buried in one of the pillows, weeping uncontrollably. She was wearing her orange dress with a large Penny Farthing printed on it in black; it was my favorite of her dresses, and I always thought she looked especially pretty in it. My parents were in the room, plainly agitated, and with that look of being lost that came upon them when there was trouble. "Go out and play in the garden," Mum said out the side of her mouth. I knew enough to do just that, and lickety-split as well. There was a fire going in the brazier outside, and I collected aphids that had started to infest my tulips, and put a tin can full of them in the fire. I looked around the shed for a while, and then inspected the tulips some more: I found a couple of slugs that needed to be thrown over the fence into the school-yard. Maybe Fergie would step on them. The tulips were never as silkily black as I wanted them to be, and always seemed to have some white ash on them, perhaps from bonfires set alight up and down the row of houses or perhaps from a mold or virus that I couldn't control. We had no sprays, and no knowledge of how to grow flowers, apart from watering them and picking off the bugs when they appeared.

"Alright, you can come in now," Mum said, despondently, at the back door, and in I went. Dad was sitting in the kitchen, with the newspaper open before him, and you could fall a thousand feet down his face; and Mum was still looking off-course. She had reached that condition where one was simply angry because one didn't know what on earth to do. Pauline had gone to her room. We ate cold leftovers, I had a slice of TV, and went to bed early. Nothing was said about what had been going on. A pall hung over the house for a few days, and I hardly saw Pauline at all. And then I forgot all about it.

A month or so later, when it had become known that the whole family was going to Australia, one of the boys I didn't like accosted me in the playground. "I know why you're goin', Jam Tart. You 'av to clear out! It's that sister of yours; she's got a bun in the oven." It was one of those moments when I stepped out-side myself and could observe myself, almost coolly, as though I were standing next to myself. "We're goin' 'cause there's layoffs at Beckton," I said, and everyone knew that the Gas Works was starting to let men go. "Yeah, then why you doin' it in a 'ole-and-corner way, that's wot I'd like to know!" the boy said, paused, and then added, "My Dad told me diff'rent." And then he stalked off. There was no birth, and nothing else, in Brisbane; and there was no telling of the secret, whatever it was, not even a word to Nan and Granddad, and certainly not a whisper in the porch to Mrs. Bray while picking up the milk. Mum, Dad, and Pauline were wrapped in a silence about something that no one could penetrate, and the silence leaked a little in sentences cut short between my parents and my sister, and showed in looks down at the carpet, and in tempers flaring more often than usual. But the event, whatever it was, was covered almost completely by the final stages of applying to be ten quid migrants, and preparing to go to Australia; and everyone, me included, took their silences, their looks, and their shortness of temper to be consequences of anxiety about the big move. Yet that afternoon of coming home from the park and being sent outside was not forgotten; it remained, like a lesion somewhere inside, and taught me, in a vague way, that a gap was being communicated to me, one that I would have to figure out by myself, if I ever could.

—— ▼ ——

One day Dad got a thick letter in a fancy envelope from Australia House that said we had been approved to go to Australia, and from that moment the future became sharply foreshortened. I was called into the living room, where Mum, Dad, and Pauline were sitting like judges on the settee (with tacked up dresses behind them, covering the mirror) and Mum announced in a hushed voice that it was a secret that we were going, but that I would be told when it was okay to tell my friends. (I knew very well that other people were in the know, even if they weren't entirely sure what was happening or exactly where we were going or why.) There was the dressmaking business to wind down, which meant working overtime to complete several wed-dings, and the money would come in handy so Mum was anx-ious that there be no cancellations through rumor that we were going; there were many forms to fill in, and there would be more trips to London; there were inoculations against diphtheria, polio, typhoid, and cholera we had to have, lest we all end up catching a rare Asian disease like Cousin Albert; and there was packing to be done, and the house to be cleaned up, both of which would take a long time.

It felt as though I was being led to the very brink of the map of all I knew and was facing a huge blank space marked "UNEX-PLORED," and the long flight to get there, I started to realize, wouldn't help to bring any of it into focus. That too was something entirely new. I had never gone further afield than Folkestone. More dazzling booklets that came in the mail from Australia House helped a little: photographs of the Botanic Gardens off Alice Street in Brisbane showed palm trees, spreading fig trees, bamboo, bougainvillea, and extravagant trees called cycads, and more photographs of beaches, especially of Surfer's Paradise on the South Coast, where brown girls and young men with rippling muscles lay side by side on white sand. Pauline particularly admired the photograph of Holy Family Catholic Church in Indooroopilly. "I'll get married there!" she said with enthusiasm. "It's Catholic, girl," Dad pointed out. "Makes no flippin' difference," she said in that independent way of hers. Mum and Dad thrilled at the pictures and at the prospect of a new life, lived in Technicolor and no longer in black and white or sepia. No drizzle in Australia, I was told, no fogs.

Eventually the time came to tell my grandparents. Mum and Dad had to go to Amesbury Road one Saturday afternoon. Pauline stayed behind to clean up her room, but I tagged along. We returned several hours later, Mum and Dad walking in ragged silence back to Rowdowns Road; the announcement had not been received well. "Wot you runnin' away for?" Granddad had said, turning round suddenly and angrily in his armchair, "Goin' on some bleedin' adventure, an' leavin' behind those who love you!" Nan just sat in her chair, crumpled by what she'd heard. The argument from unemployment was put to him, but it made

no impression on him and Nan. "Jim can find anovver soddin'
job round 'ere somewhere. There'll be places lookin' for someone not afraid o' a 'ard day's bloody work." But the die had been
cast, and now that everyone in the immediate family had seen its
dots in plain daylight, I was given to understand that I could tell
my friends. I told Kevin and Eddie, who were hurt, less because
I was leaving than because I had kept it a secret. "My Mum and
Dad said I wasn't to tell anyone!" I defended myself. "But you
could 'av told us!" Eddie said, looking away, with conviction and
with reason. At Eastbrook I had to give my homeroom teacher a
note saying when I would be leaving. "Off to Australia, are we?"
he said more to himself than to me and with, I thought, a wistful
expression. "Well, I'll have a report drawn up for you before you
go." On my last lunch there it was so raw that I could not hold
the metal spoon in my right hand, and so couldn't eat the pudding and hot custard. "I'll remember this all my life," I said to
myself, as I looked out of a grimy window. Even the sleety snow
looked gray.

I had fully expected that our dog Kim and our cat Bobbie
would be coming with us, but one day Mum told me that they
would be going to two other families. I burst into tears. "You
wouldn't want 'em to go all that way in crates with luggage
all around 'em," she said, "they wouldn't like it and they'd get
sick." "They'd 'ave to stay in quarantine for *months*," Dad added.
"Can't they go with *Nan*, then?" I tried, with desperation in my
voice. "Nah, they don't want 'em," Mum said brutally, "she's got
enough on 'er hands with Snowy. Either we give 'em away or we
'av to put 'em to sleep." "We've already sold Charlie; someone's
comin' to pick 'im up on Tuesday." It was a *fait accompli*; I felt
that I had been tricked, and I saw, more clearly than I had before,
heartlessness only thinly covered by sentiment in both of them.
Our pets had only ever been living toys for them. As soon as they
became inconvenient, they had to go.

Eventually, the suitcases were packed; they all looked over-weight, and Dad had to sit on them so that Mum or Pauline could lock them. "Wot'll we do if we 'av to open 'em at the air-port?" was a recurring question. There were Authorities there, too. "If anyone wants to open mine," Pauline said, "he can bloody well close it up again, that's all I'll say." My days in Lon-don were quickly petering out, and the last two or three could only be lived halfway, if that. At least I had finished with East-brook. The report I took home, in a sealed brown envelope, read, "Kevin is an itelligent boy but lacks confidence. He must work hard in order to realize that he has some ability." Dad showed it to me, with a dismal expression on his face. I pointed out the spelling mistake, which made me feel a little better but didn't change his downcast look. The last night we spent at Nan and Granddad's. Mum slept with Nan and Pauline in one bed, and Granddad and Dad slept in another bed, while I had the spare bed upstairs to myself. It was one of the best nights' rest that I had ever had. It was January, bitter, and my bed was heaped with blankets. Nan fried up a breakfast, though Mum couldn't eat. "'ave a bit of black puddin', girl," Nan said flatly, "Need to keep your strength up, goin' all that way." Then we all walked up Gale Street to Becontree Station, cocooned in our jumpers, coats, overcoats, and scarfs, Granddad carrying two suitcases and smoking his pipe, and as we got close Pauline began to weep. "Too late for that, girl," Nan said, "Too bleedin' late for that."

4 ▶

I wanted to linger at the very top of the staircase to the plane that would fly us from London to Sydney, and take a long, melancholy farewell look at the city I would never see again. I told Dad of my Romantic intention, and he said not to be so daft, since I'd hold up the whole boarding process. The plane, a Boeing 707, was so long it tapered as I looked down it; it had two seats on either side of an aisle, and we quickly formed ourselves into a little square. We were hardly over the Channel, it seemed, when we were told that breakfast would be served. There was a menu in the seat pocket, and in a script with many swirls and paraphs it announced *Omelette tomate*. Ah, French food at last! A tomato omelet would surely be red, but when it came it was yellow. Perhaps they forgot to mix in the tomato, I thought, a little punctured, but as soon as I cut the omelet tomato gushed out like hot blood. I had never tasted anything so good. We jumped and bumped and twisted our way down the globe, stopping to refuel in Frankfort, Beirut, Kuwait, Karachi, Kuala Lumpur, and Hong Kong, and with each leg ate one or more meals, each seemingly better than the last. I slept through two of them, despite my best intentions. There was a bruising thunderstorm over Beirut when we were descending, and we kept going down, up, around, and then down again, all of which agonized Dad whose ears were hurting badly, despite the amount of barley sugar he sucked, and who kept his eyes firmly shut the whole time. His anxiety level was through the roof, especially when lightning jabbed near the plane, and would have been through a roof much higher than the one actually over our heads.

Eventually, after two days of being up in the air, we arrived in Darwin. It was in the early hours of the morning, and we groped to the exit half asleep. Outside, darkness: perhaps one of those vast patches marked "UNEXPLORED" on the map, then, looking to one side, a few faint lights far away. As I walked down the mobile staircase, wearing a jumper and coat and carrying my overcoat, the steamy air enveloped me; and when I was on the tarmac it settled somewhere about my chest as though I were wading through a warm pool. It seemed to take forever to reach the open hangar where we were led. Once there, we were pointed to several trestle tables, each with a narrow grid of tall glasses of lemon water. By then rivulets of sweat were pouring from me, and I must have drunk two or three glasses of the lemon water before we were led back into the plane, limper than when we had arrived an hour or two before. What had happened? We had touched the very tip of Australia, had felt its strangeness for a moment, and then were returned to the world. Yet when I woke, approaching Sydney, it could have been a dream, an unsettling one that would never go away.

We overshot Sydney. Dad looked out and saw that we were no longer flying over houses but tightly creased water and said, "'ere, the pilot's missed the city!" He was anxious until the plane turned round to approach the airport. I could see little boats unzipping the water on Botany Bay, and then Sydney started to sprawl beneath us: a city built on land colored a hungry green with endless red rooftops and occasional patches of blue that made no sense until I realized that they were swimming pools. The city center sprouted tightly in the distance. We'd be going up to Brisbane by train, and so it couldn't be more than an hour or so away. I thought how at a pinch I could cycle down to Sydney, and explore it, just as I had done with Eastbrookland. I could see that there were parks, big ones. As I was daydreaming about that, Mum leaned over and said, "You'll 'av a week off, an' then you go back to school. You gotta do better 'ere. Understand?" I nodded because I understood all right, but I drew a blank when I wondered how I could do better. Maybe school would be easier here. I'd been told that life in Australia was more easygoing than in England. It certainly was a relief to feel that with each moment of the trip I was getting further and further away from Thomas Arnold and Eastbrook; but where on earth was I going? The question finally bit. For the first time, I felt that there was no ground under my feet.

At Customs in Sydney my picnic basket of birds eggs was taken from me; it was going to be incinerated. I wasn't all that upset, since I'd planned to donate it to the Museum in Brisbane, which I imagined to be a smaller version of the London Museum but sadly without any specimens of robin eggs and chaffinch eggs. The Director of the Museum would receive the gift from me with many thanks. Then they would appear in a glass case with a small white card, "Gift of Kevin Hart, Esq." Besides, I knew there were birds in Queensland, large and small ones, all in exotic colors. I had seen pictures of them in those glistening booklets that came from Australia House. Having cleared Customs, we learned that, since we had arrived on the Australia Day holiday, there was no train for us and we'd be flown to Brisbane; and so we approached another city, one up north, by water so blue it went straight to my head, like drinking icy water far too quickly, though the green on the land seemed dark here and there and half-starved in other places. We turned towards the Brisbane River and followed it, almost lazily, for a long stretch, the plane lilting slightly this way and then that.

What was this city beneath me? It didn't seem as burnished as in the photographs, and I felt disappointed that we weren't going to live in Sydney. Well, that's where I would go if I were to run away again! (After half an hour in the air I knew it was far too far away to cycle there for weekend adventures, but I could always catch a train and vanish there.) We had to wait for the mobile staircase to be brought out to the plane, and when I started to walk down it I gripped the right-hand metal handrail. My hand leapt back, burned. The staircase must have been left out for hours in the punishing sun. I was carrying my overcoat, and soon was carrying my jacket and jumper on top of it. My winter trousers itched, and again I was dripping with sweat in the hot wet air. Then we were inside. There we all were, standing in a little group in the airport, our obese suitcases surrounding us, with lost expressions on our faces, somewhere on the other side of the world, waiting for an unknown man to meet us. I kept disappearing into the toilet to run cold water over the palm of my right hand.

—— ▼ ——

Eventually a heavyset man came. He was wearing a felt hat with a broad brim, set quite a way back on his head, and he was dabbing his forehead with a handkerchief. "You the Pom family?" he asked, offering a good-natured smile. Taking a suitcase easily in each hand, he led us to his station wagon in the parking lot. We drove southwest, skimming suburbs with peculiar names. Auchenflower: was it named for all its flowers, especially, perhaps, a local flower presumably called the "Auchen"? (Dad said he thought there was a place in Scotland with the same name, so letting the air out of my theory.) Indooroopilly: its name must have been stretched when left out in the heat. (I kept that one to myself.) Every now and again the Brisbane River would appear, gleaming, to the left. After forty minutes or so the houses were thinning out quite quickly, we were entering the more distant suburbs that eventually would fray into bush or, if you followed the railway line, lead to Ipswich, and finally the houses just stopped dead in the heat and we drove along a stretch of highway that simply cut through the bush and came to an empty, dusty place called Wacol.

We passed an army barracks and turned into the migrant hostel where we would be staying until we found a house. There was row on row of small wooden huts, arranged alphabetically into blocks, and also larger Nissen huts made of corrugated iron. Dropped off at an administration building, and all too dazed by jet lag, heat, and information, we were pointed to a shower block and told we could take a shower once a day (back home I'd had a bath once a week), a communal laundry, a convenience store, a canteen where meals were served three times a day, and I saw what looked to be a playground. No sooner were we out of the car, though, than mosquitoes whined around and about. It was hot, sticky, and gritty, and we were all a stop or two beyond exhaustion. We were led to one of the wooden huts, passing women walking slowly along with children, all in thongs or barefoot, and were left there to unpack our luggage. Dad opened the door; Mum looked into the stifling space with its bare furnishing and collapsed in tears. "Oh Jim, wot *'ave* we *done?*" she wailed, maybe recalling the Nissen huts in West Ham, built by Italian prisoners of war and still there two decades later. Somewhere a radio was playing "Georgy Girl."

I left the three of them to recover, and went out to explore our quarter and a bit further. I went into the shower block: wet concrete and a snarling smell of disinfectant. I heard a kookaburra for the first time, and saw that a tall mesh wire fence ran around the whole hostel; beyond it, nothing but gum trees, which were densely inhabited by birds and Lord knows what else. At first it seemed to be another caravan holiday, though far away from any beach, then differences became apparent: inside, white nets like bridal veils lying limply over the beds—what were they for? — and outside, incessant magpie calls (as I quickly learned) and that acrid smell was DDT (as I heard a day or two later). We went to the canteen for our first dinner: families sitting down with meals on metal trays, and huge fans languidly casting about the room, vainly trying to cool it down. The next day, at lunch, the world was slowly beginning to ratchet into place. For children there was an "Oslo Lunch": a slice of white bread and margarine, a stick of cheese in plastic wrap, a couple of leaves of lettuce, half a tomato, a twisted slice or two of orange, and a glass of milk. I'd never had orange for lunch before. I imagined how good life must be for children growing up in Oslo, a city I'd seen on the atlas at school. It must be cool there, I thought, as I looked outside and saw the blue sky shimmering outside. Incredibly, the day was getting hotter even as we ate.

—— ▼ ——

After a couple of decent nights' sleep, more oblivion than sleep, we recovered, more or less, and immediately there was concern over where Dad was to get work. We were miles from anywhere! It was absolutely forbidden to do unauthorized work in the camp. A few men and women got jobs in the canteen, or as cleaners, but that was clearly a recipe for living for a couple of years in the camp. Some families did, and you could see misery deepen in the faces of the women who had to persuade themselves that the wooden hut was home away from home or in long prospect of home. Often they simply saved up what they could and then went back to Britain. Overhearing their conversations in the queue for lunch or dinner, you could tell that their grand adventure had become merely a loop in lives of disappointment. Mum and Dad were determined to stay in Brisbane, no matter what, and one night after dinner Mum leaned over to Dad and whispered that she'd run up a few dresses in the hut—she had been clever enough to bring her baby Elna sewing machine with her, after all—and we would get by that way until Dad could bring in some money. She had to be careful, though. There were Authorities here, too, and who knows if one of them might be walking past our hut and see what was going on? In a week or two, the hut had a couple of simple florals hanging in Mum and Dad's bedroom, where no Authority was likely to see them. "If anyone sees anythin'," she whispered, "I'll just say that they're mine. They won't know the difference!" She had forgotten that the florals were for young slim girls, and these days it looked as though she had been blown up at the navel with a bicycle pump.

I made sure that no one saw me when I walked to the end of the camp and slipped through one of the gates in the mesh-wire fence into the bush beyond. There were signs in red capital letters sternly forbidding anyone to enter the area, though why was unclear to me. Once through a gate, the bush was immediately dense, invisibly packed with cicadas singing, magpies calling, and kookaburras making their mocking cries. They were supposed to sound like laughter, I remembered from the booklets from Australia House, but they seemed far less reassuring than that. With no track, it was next to impossible to make my way through the bush, but I managed to zigzag through, and half an hour later the bush was exactly the same as it was when brushing up against the fence. No birds could be seen, but mosquitoes could certainly be felt. My arms were a bumpy mess already. The whole place had a strong scent of oil. Then I saw before me a huge insect immobile on the trunk of a tree; it had claws, and looked like one of those blown glass knick-knacks on our mantel piece back home, and yet at the same time it was otherworldly. For a moment or two, I couldn't move. I got close enough to see that it was hollow, but it was scary all the same. "Don't go any further," it said. I turned around; but I had zigged and zagged a lot, and everywhere I looked around me, the bush repeated itself without error. Easing past all the branches that had stuck in my

way there, I hadn't broken anything, and so had no traces to follow back.

I turned around, pushing back through the bush, faster now,
scratching my legs and arms as I went, and sweating hard, but
seemed to get nowhere. There was no fence to see, and the
huts were too low to be glimpsed though the thick bush. I was
getting thirsty, although I'd had a glass or two of milk at breakfast, making the most of something I could never have had so
much of back home. Thick yellow sunlight pounded relentlessly
through the gums, which offered hardly any shade, even though
they grew close together, and I hadn't yet been given a hat to
wear. The first wave of panic came over me, soaking me. Could
I be lost after only half an hour? Not even at Eastbrookland did
things ever come to that. A kookaburra cried out somewhere
above me. The heat was making my head swim, but surely I was
heading in the right direction. In the end, I saw the fence glinting
dully through the trees; and it turned out that I was at the opposite end of the camp. I followed the fence until I found a gate,
pushed my hand through the mesh to get the latch, hurting my
wrist in the process, then slipped back in, late for lunch, where
I drank glass after glass of cold water. "Wot you been doin'?"
Mum asked, taking in my red face and sweat-stained shirt. "Just
lookin' round," I said. "Yeah, it's bloody hot in this 'ere country,"
she said, looking very fed-up.

One respite from the endless heat and humidity, we were told
by a Dutch family in the next hut, was watermelon. We didn't
know what this was but bought one anyway from a man who
drove into the camp one day and had a ton of them on the back
of his ute. It was bigger and rounder than a rugby ball. Mum cut
off the very end, and a tiny bit of red showed. "Who wants a
slice?" she asked, triumphantly, wielding a long knife. Gingerly,
I licked the red bit, which was chill and delicious, but all too
thin. Then she cut another slice, in which there was far more red

stuff, and Dad had that. Then Pauline got her slice. Soon enough I got a proper slice as well. "Bloody pips," Mum said, when she started on hers. Then some juice dripped on her dress. She stood up quickly, knocking the table, and the watermelon rolled off, bumped heavily on the floor, and split. The knife fell too, just missing her foot. "Bloody stupid watermelon!" she exclaimed. Up early the next day, I saw the truncated melon in the garbage bin. Ants were swarming all over it. I knew what I'd hear soon, if I stayed around: "Bloody stupid ants!"

——— ▼ ———

So I started to go to school again, this time to Goodna State School. Mum had taken me there a day or two before, and in the Headmaster's office I was assigned a class. There was a disagreement between the Headmaster and Mum as to how old I was. She told him I was eleven, as I was, but he begged to differ and, counting on his fingers from July 1954, the month and year of my birth, declared me to be ten and therefore should go into Grade Six. Mum fumed all the way home on the train, but an Authority is an Authority, and one simply does not dispute with them. Now, early on a Monday morning, I was waiting for the school bus with the other kids in the camp. It arrived, and we scrambled in. Most of the boys who had been in the camp for a while went to school in khaki shorts and bare feet; the girls wore skirts and sandals or thongs. I was the only boy wearing long trousers, shoes and socks.

It must have been the oldest bus in the world: the seats had no cushions and no seatbelts, something I'd seen only in the plane and in a couple of cars, the bus had no suspension, and the whole thing seemed to have been made out of thin plates of rusted steel painted dirty yellow. There were leftover scraps of lunch from the week before on the back seats, a cat must have been in there over the weekend and had peed in the aisle, and every surface had been scribbled on, carved, chipped or scraped by a generation or two of kids going back and forth to school. If anything, the bus driver was even older and more broken down. He was thin, sun darkened, with sunken cheeks and white stubble all over his face and neck. He started up the bus, which shook violently, and jolted it into first gear. We turned into the Ipswich Road, and lurched, each time the driver changed gears, for fifteen minutes until we arrived at the school. Taciturn, the driver didn't seem bothered by the boys carrying on all over the bus, giving one another "burns" or seeing who could pick off the most sunburned skin before getting to school. The girls sat on one side of the bus, staying entirely separate from the boys, vessels of oil and water.

There were two grade six classes, and I was put into the female teacher's room. Both classes were upstairs, for the whole school was on stilts, as if it might be taking off into space, though the downstairs area was being closed in that year to make more classrooms. The school was growing because of the increasing number of kids from Wacol. "You're lucky," said the boy who was sitting next to me on the bus as we climbed the stairs and he turned into the room next door. Why was he so forlorn? The answer became clear soon enough. Blonde, curly, and curvy, and with a face that was pretty when she was relaxed and hard when she wasn't, which was most of the time, my new teacher pointed me to a desk in the middle of the room, and immediately we started the first lesson of the morning. No introductions: new kids from the Wacol camp were all too common at Goodna; we would come and we would go, and the only constant community was the local kids, most of whom wore white shirts and khaki shorts or patterned cotton dresses. The locals appeared neat; the kids from the hostel, ragged.

For the first lesson, the teacher drew quotation marks about three feet long on the blackboard. "Do you remember what these are?" she asked us all in a high nasal voice that didn't go with her fragile looks. A blonde girl put up her hand: "Sixty-six and ninety-nine!" she said, happily. It turned out that when opening a quotation one used sixty-six and when closing it one used ninety-nine. I had been taught quotation marks at Thomas Arnold a couple of years before, but they were no more than a sparrow's footprints before and after a quotation, with no shape to them at all, and certainly with none of the attention to curve and incline that our teacher had devoted to them on the board. We had to write down several sentences she'd put up in chalk, each quoting direct speech, and then Miss came round each desk to check on our work. *"Kevin Hart,"* she said with mock horror when leaning over my shoulder (the mixture of her deodorant, scent, and face powder was almost overpowering), "I don't think I've ever seen worse handwriting!" (Pause.) *"Did you never do Copy Book?"* I had never heard of the expression, and I shook my head. "Well, you will here!" she said, decisively. "Is that a fountain pen you have?" (Another pause while she took in the dire fact.) "Well, put it away, and use this pencil for today; tomorrow you can bring a biro."

There was a door on the far left between the two classes, and the sporty male sixth grade teacher, Mr. Greg O'Kane, had the other room. He would assign work to his class, and then lean in the doorway at the back of his room, flexing his shoulders and looking at our teacher, occasionally taking in his and then our class in a swiveling panoptic gaze. Once in a while, I was told at lunch that day, he would throw a stick of chalk or a blackboard eraser at any boy in either class who wasn't paying attention, and his aim was true. If he heard noise in our room, he would appear with a three-foot blackboard ruler in his hand and would slap it against his leg. He was supposedly keeping an eye on our teacher because she was young and inexperienced, though it took no time at all to work out that his eye was highly attentive to her legs. She often wore a red skirt, which came to within two or two and a half inches of her knees, but every so often she had to bend over a desk to check on a child's work and these were moments that Mr. O'Kane must have cherished. Sometimes he simply stepped into the room and walked around, or picked on a child to answer a question, and then withdrew to his own class-room. Sometimes you could hear him whistling "Friday on my Mind."

"I'm glad I'm not in O'Kane's class," I said at lunchtime to a boy fated to be in the other room as we got out our yo-yos. "He's not so bad," he said. "He's a lot more fun than the old sour puss you got." True enough, once a week on Friday afternoons we would hear great crashes, hoots and yells coming from the room next door. Mr. O'Kane had orchestrated a battle between two halves of the class! Sometimes, if you were seated close enough, you could see through the door: kids running back and forth, breathless, falling over, laughing, and getting tagged. It lasted all of fifteen minutes, and in that time Miss would simply stop, sit at her desk with a prim expression, and wait it out. "Open your books and read," she would say, and we would open our books; but no one could read or wanted to. "Can *we* have a battle too, Miss?" one of the Wacol boys asked. "There will be no battles in *this* classroom," she said decisively.

Teaching under surveillance, and undoubtedly all too aware of the O'Kanian gaze, must have given our teacher a perpetual headache, for she did something I had never seen before. Every couple of hours she would take a little envelope from a box, open it, bring it to her lips and swallow pink crystals. I could see the name on the white and yellow package that was always on her desk: *Vincent's Powders*. Later, when we had rented a TV at home, I would see them advertised between programs; the jingle said that the powders offer "three-way" relief (by way of aspirin, phenacetin, and caffeine). "Take a Vincent's with a cup of tea

and lie down" was common advice that Brisbane women gave
one another when things got too much with the heat and kids;
and it was years before the powders were found to be addictive
and associated with kidney failure. My teacher must have been
relieved when Mr. O'Kane took both classes outside after the
first couple of lessons for "little lunch."

The ritual of little lunch revolved around just one thing: the
consumption of free milk supplied by the State Government of
Queensland, presumably so as to generate healthy young citizens of the Sunshine State. Before the bell went, the milk mon-
itor disappeared downstairs. Then, when it went, we assembled
there as well, on a slab of concrete, Mr. O'Kane making sure that
we formed ourselves into exact rows of boys and girls. Then we
had to walk past a wire crate and take a third of a pint of milk with
a straw, and then, I learned, we had to drink it all, while walking
continuously and quickly in formation. The milk must have been
left out in the remorseless January sun for hours, and the bottle top was hard to pierce with the straw. Most of us pushed in
the top with our thumbs, which for some reason was forbidden,
and then inserted the straw. The first taste was truly horrible:
the milk was lumpy, warm and sour, but Mr. O'Kane was vigi-
lant that it was all drunk in only a few minutes. Then, sick in the
stomach, I put the empty bottle back into the crate, along with
the punctured top, trooped back up the stairs to the hot classroom, and Mr. O'Kane languidly resumed his post between the
two rooms. I noticed that *he* hadn't had any of the milk.

The school day eventually clanged to an end, and the bus was
waiting at the gate along with its driver who looked no better in
the afternoon than he did in the morning. We all piled into the
wreck, which became overfull because of kids who had missed
the bus in the morning and had had to come by train or in a
borrowed car; a few of us had to stand at the back, and then it
swayed onto the road. After a few minutes, though, it ground to a

halt. "Youse kids wait a bit," the driver said out of the side of his mouth, not looking at any of us, "an' don't get out the bus." He disappeared into a building just off the roadside with *XXXX* over it. Five minutes passed, then a few more, and then quite a few more; it was fetid in the bus, and only one window was open, and only because it was broken. We fanned ourselves with exercise books. "Wot's he doin' in there?" I asked one of the grade seven boys. "He goes into the pub and has a coupla pots on the way back," he said, "happens every day." And so it did. But we all got back to the camp, though once he skidded on the gravel making a turn. I told my parents over dinner at night, as part of the story of my first day at the new school. They raised their eyebrows, but said nothing. "'e must be imaginin' it," they were thinking, "just couldn't 'appen." Or were they thinking, "Best not upset the apple cart, we'll be out of 'ere before long"?

———▾———

After a day or two, we had a test to make sure that we still remembered what we had learned the previous year. "Well, we'll see what you know," teacher said crisply, when I pointed out that I hadn't been there a week. So we lined up outside the class-room, went in, and each found a test on our desk. "Start now," Miss said, "and remember to cover your work!" (That meant to write with your left-arm sheltering the paper so no one else could see it.) I turned it over, and could answer the first ques-tion, but no sooner had I started writing, with my sister's bic, than the boy to my right caught my attention and made me look up. There was a black hairy spider, about a hand's width, on the ceiling, right above my head! Instinctively, I shot up and moved away, knocking over my chair. "What are you *doing*?" Miss cried when she spun around to see what was making the commotion. I was too scared of the spider to say anything, but just pointed to it. "Oh *that*," she said, "it's more scared of you than you are of it."

(That hardly seemed possible.) "But wot if it *falls?*" "Well, then it'll go down the back of your shirt!" she said. (Endless laughter in the class.) Mr. O'Kane suddenly appeared at the doorway with his blackboard ruler. "Get back to your tests!" she said sharply, as if someone else had made the joke. "And you, get back to your seat." The spider clung to the ceiling and never moved. I looked up every few seconds, and did little of the test.

In that first summer in Brisbane I seemed to be out in the yard or in the field for two or three afternoons each week. There was "Marching" twice a week. This was something new. We were arranged into square blocks of boys and girls, and had to march in highly stylized way—arms rigid and going up to the level of the chin—for half an hour back and forth before Mr. O'Kane. It didn't take him very long to realize that I was usually out of step with the others, so he plucked me from the line and tried to teach me how to march in time. He showed me, clearly enough, and I tried to imitate him; and then I was allowed to return to my division of kids. No sooner was I back than I was out of step again, making a mess of the whole thing. Mr. O'Kane tried again; and again I was out of step. Eventually, I was taken out of the square and told to watch from the sideline. "Can't see marchin' workin' in a London school," I thought to myself, as I stood watching the class go back and forth, back and forth. Then I remembered a Christmas play at Thomas Arnold where I had been cast as one of the three kings, and was taken to Benfield's office for a remedial lesson in how to walk in an appropriately stately manner. All the same, I was already rehabilitating my months at Eastbrook, and missing playing hide and seek in the smog. Even the Tattoo to which Granddad had taken me started to assume a warm glow in memory.

I was on the cricket field for two afternoons each week; perhaps there was a big game for which the class needed practice or, more likely, there just wasn't enough one could do with sleepy

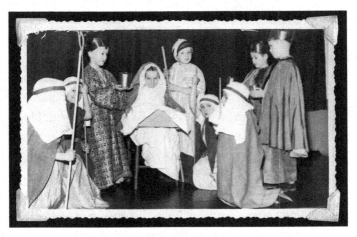

Christmas play

children in class. Kids from the camp were a rootless society, always on the way somewhere else, and our education would start properly in that other school on the other side of town, down the coast, or even back in England. How could Goodna ever compete properly? I never stayed in long as a batsman, and I had endless time in the outfield; time would stall out there, go slowly round and round in a circle, while the scene before me went grainy every so often, trees shimmering in the distance, and cicadas droning on and on. Once in a while a boy would faint. "Run along and get a drink at the tap," Mr. O'Kane would say, almost kindly, when he came to pick him up. He was always at his best out in the field. And the barefoot boy would run off, drink, splash himself with cold water, and troop back into the unforgiving sun for another hour or more of cricket. Only once did a ball ever dribble out to my part of the outfield, and when it did it seemed as though I was hallucinating it. I threw it back, and then time stopped once again for another half hour.

A black figure started wobbling towards us from the school. As the distorted shape got closer to us, Mr. O'Kane saw who was coming, and brought the game to a sudden halt. It was the

Headmaster, old Jack Heber, who would sometimes break in on classes and take over. "C'mon boys," he said, "form a circle and sit down." And so we did. He stood there, tall, thin, erect, with black trousers and a black jacket, sweaty white shirt and a black tie. His face was a web of wrinkles beneath a brutal crew cut. "You kids don't know anything about the Japs," he suddenly said, out of the blue. "They had some of our blokes in camps up there," he said, "when we lost Malaya; they were just bags of bones by the end." He paused, looking around the field with intense, empty eyes. "You there, son, run and get me a chair!" Soon it appeared, but he didn't sit on it, as I thought he would. He stood and put his right foot on it, and continued to ramble on about the Japs in the war. Mr. O'Kane stood there, arms folded, with a look that was somewhere between indulgent and worried, until the bell leapt across the field. "Run along boys," Heber said. "Have a drink at the tap, and get on home." Sitting in the bus, I could see him standing out in the field, buttonholing Mr. O'Kane, his foot still on the chair.

———— ▼ ————

We were ten or eleven years old in Grade Six, and the room was an endlessly crosshatched space of glimpses and glances going back and forth. This hadn't been so in London: was it because of the heat, or the new, slightly more relaxed world I was in, or because I was a few months older? I looked to left or right to see what Billy or Ian was doing, sometimes because one of them was glancing emptily at me, simply as a way of punctuating the story he was writing; over to the right, near the windows looking over the corridor, to check out those pretty blonde twins whose skin was honey, and who never looked back, intent as they were with their schoolwork; right to the front wall to note the time on the big white clock the hands of which never seemed to move; up to the ceiling to make sure there was no spider there; out of the window that framed huge gum trees that shimmered and broke up in the heat haze; around and about to see where the teacher was and if she was coming my way (when she was I could smell her deodorant and feel her knowing glance on the back of my neck); and always to the partition to check whether Mr. O'Kane was there, what he might have in his hand and whether he had his eye on me. Glances veered off faces, hair, globe, windows, teachers walking past in the corridor, clock, and blackboard, slipped off sweaty arms ahead of me, and returned to caress the cheeks, hair, and legs of those blonde girls by the wall.

The twins were Australian girls, wearing identical check cotton dresses, and seemed endlessly happy to be in school and to sit together. They must have been swimmers, since they were suntanned more deeply and evenly than anyone else. When they smiled, which was almost all the time, their teeth were straight and white, unlike anything else I had ever seen. They never mixed with any of the boys, but ate their small triangular sandwiches, trimmed of crusts, by themselves with tiny, considered bites a few yards away from the other girls who sat on the benches near the taps. Every so often the dress of the girl closer to me would get caught up a little, and my glance was a secret touch from several desks away, repeated as often as I dared. Having grown up with girls, older than I was to be sure, sitting in knickers and bra night after night, and having heard their conversation for years, I wasn't scared of them. I enjoyed their company and felt at ease with them. So one day, as we were all pouring out to lunch, I went with the twins down the stairs, planning to sit with them. They weren't identical twins in every respect, and there were many opportunities to ponder which of the two was the prettier. When my intention became apparent, right at the bottom of the stairs when one had to turn this way or that, one of the twins said, decisively, but with one of those glittering smiles, "*We* eat lunch over there, just the two of us" and they walked together softly in that direction, as they always did. "Wot you wanna 'ave lunch with *girls* for?" a new boy from London in the camp asked me. I thought it was obvious, but when I tried to explain the appeal of that honey skin, those white teeth, those sandals, those curving legs, and their air of happiness, the words didn't come. "Like one of my banana sandwiches?" I asked instead. "I'll 'ave one of your Fig Newtons," he replied.

On the weekends my parents thought it a duty to explore this alien place with its bleaching sun where they had decided to live the rest of their lives. Mostly it was a matter of getting to know the suburbs nearby, since it was an unspoken truth that we wouldn't venture far afield: how could we ever get to know Moorooka, Mount Gravatt, or Nundah? But we could visit Darra, Oxley, and Corinda, since they were all just a short train ride away. Sometimes I fantasized that Dad would come home one day and announce that he'd got a job out west in Dalby or Roma or, even better, Thargomindah or Birdsville, the latter two surely bordering on huge tracts of land marked "UNEXPLORED." If we were going to come all the way here, we might as well go all the way when here. Instead, we trudged on scorching, airless days along the bedraggled streets of Darra, which was one stop away from Wacol, taking stock of houses, especially those for sale. On our first trip there, Mum saw a tiny house with some chooks running about it on a dirt road not far from the station. "That'd do for me, Jim," she said, nodding at it, with a hint of braveness in her voice. Her expectations of life in the new land had diminished massively in just a few weeks. I thought: we've come all this way for *this*? What happened to chicken salad on the beach? On other weekends we ventured as far as Sherwood to do the same trawling and to sit in similar milk bars for cups of tea and chiko rolls (and a Polly Waffle for me if things were going well), and it became evident that the further one went from Wacol towards Central the better Brisbane was; but to enter that barely lower middle-class world Dad needed a job, and sooner rather than later.

Amazingly, Dad got a job as a "postie," riding a bike around Sherwood and Corinda, and blowing a whistle when he put the letters into a box by the gate. I had never imagined him doing anything like this; in fact, I had never imagined him being visible in his work. He never was while at Beckton. Within a few weeks he was dark brown and a few pounds lighter. He was the slowest man on the job; more, he was always exhausted when he got home. No sooner was he out on his round than he started to sweat heavily, and soon he became dehydrated. "Can I 'av a glass of water, Missis?" was his constant refrain on his route, and the answers weren't always positive or even polite, especially when he asked if he could use their dunny. Women in long, loose floral frocks would emerge from behind milky mosquito nets on the verandahs of Queenslanders, and either return with a glass of water or tell him to be on his way. He stuck with it for a few months, and I think that if it had been much longer he would have collapsed while pedaling uphill on a fiery day. One afternoon, when he got back to the home base, he had to be taken to a doctor who, when he checked Dad's blood pressure, genially said that he couldn't understand how he was still alive. He told Mum in their bedroom around five, just when we were about to go for an early dinner. Through the doorway I could see Mum's face go slack. She said something I couldn't hear, and then blew her nose. "Best get somethin' to eat," she said. "Where *are* you, Kevin?"

I was lying on my bed, under the mosquito net with a singed mosquito coil on the little table nearby, and gazing at the white world around me, the net moving every so often when the fan rotated and caught its hem in its breeze. A shadow had fallen, but how dark it was and how long it would last I could not tell. A nail in my parents' future had become loose, and perhaps the whole thing would start to fall apart. If Dad got really sick, maybe we'd have to return to England. Australia was probably only for healthy people; we had all had medical examinations before being given the green light to come here, after all. Eastbrook took a giant's step closer. "And you thought you had escaped!" that short teacher with the long cane said to me, laughing. I got off my bed and joined them on a silent walk to the canteen.

By the time we went to dinner that day it was later than usual, and before we had finished eating, the daily thunderstorm had grumbled into view. It massed overhead in glowering clouds, dark gray and green like a blackbird's eggs; gusts of wind started bothering the camp, picking up sheets of newspaper left on benches and twirling loose bits of bark and twigs. The entire camp went dark. Then came a spasm of lightning, followed by a great crack of thunder, as though the sky had actually been split. Rain lashed the huts. We watched from the canteen door, seeing great horses of wind charge around, knocking into huts and trees, turning over dustbins, and the sky uncovering and unleashing a seething power always there but just hidden by the pitiless blue of summer. Thick ropes of rain were hanging from a broken gutter not far from the door. Then there were hailstones the size of peas pinging high on metal bins and roofs. After half an hour it was all over. Dad was relieved, and we walked back to our hut, through the cooler air and the raw smell of earth and gum leaves, our thongs flopping about in pools of water. I picked up a hailstone the size of a ripe plum.

Perhaps because of that scare about Dad's health it was decided that our weekends wouldn't involve trudging around the suburbs so much. At least there was a bit of money coming in. Once we took a ferry to Dunwich on North Stradbroke Island, just a little way from Brisbane. I had never been on a ferry before, and greatly liked standing on the side of the boat having the ragged wind ruffle my hair and looking out for dolphins, which I had read could sometimes be seen on the way there. As we approached, Dunwich seemed fragile, perched there on the very edge of an island, but on arriving it became surprisingly real, as though I'd crossed from one style of life to another. So I could live here, I thought to myself, and started to imagine what it would be like to live on the island, facing Moreton Bay. What would I do all day? Work in one of the shops, I suppose. There didn't seem to be anything else to do, apart from do something or other on the ferry. Docking, it became apparent that my parents had no idea what on earth to do on the island, and of course houses for sale there were of no interest at all. "S'pose we just walk around and 'av a look," Dad said, to which Mum responded, "Must be somewhere we can get a cuppa tea."

So we walked up Oxley Parade and Flinders Avenue, then along Bingle Road, and looked out across Moreton Bay towards Brisbane. And we had a cup of tea and some burned sultana toast. Later, walking round the beach, we bought some yellow grapes; they held summer tightly in their skins. After that, it was an hour before the ferry returned to the mainland, and Mum and Dad wanted to wait by the dock. "Don't wanna miss the ferry!" they kept saying, now brightly and now as if it were a matter of life and death. Standing there, in the salty light, I saw down on the beach five or six teenagers splashing in the water. Three of them were girls in bikinis with the same honey skin as the twins at school. I instantly felt a sharp pang of regret that I didn't know them, would never know them, and could never be part of their world. They were happy, swimming freely about like porpoises; and their laughter almost sounded like an accusation of timidity and stubbornness in my ears. I would have to change so that I could be with them or with others like them before I was too much older. But how does one change?

— ▼ —

After a few months, Mum and Dad found a house in Oxley—
Oxley *Heights*, Mum liked to say—and we left the camp. When
we first looked over the house I saw a little sentry box out the
back, and went to look at it. It had a seat in it, and smelled of
something I'd learn was creosote. "Wot's that?" Mum asked the
man showing us around when she saw it from the kitchen window. "The Dunny?" he asked. "Eh?" "Oh, it's the *Dunny*. This
area ain't got no sewerage yet." It turned out that once a week
the Dunnyman came around and cleared away the refuse. It also
turned out that when you went out there at night with a torch
you sometimes found a hairy spider hanging on the wall.

We brought a cat with us. I had been home one day with one
of those bugs that circulated rapidly in the hostel, and had heard
a scratching at the door of the hut. A black kitten was there with
large, intense green eyes, and she walked right in, mewed, and
licked my foot. I gave her a saucer of milk, and when Mum came
home she could see at once that we were inseparable. I named
her Sooty. Step aside Bébert, Jeoffry and Hodge, and you too
Pangur Bán, and give pride of place to an orphan feline from the
southwest suburbs of Brisbane! Never was there a more loyal or
more loving cat. She would sleep on my bed, sharing my pillow,
and sit purring on my lap whenever I settled in an armchair; she
would walk with me to school and meet me at the school gate
at the end of the day; she would bring me gifts of dead mice she
caught under the house, and leave them at the back door in a
straight row; she would sit on my little desk, making sure that I
did my homework (sometimes knocking pens and pencils and
rubbers onto the floor to keep me alert in the afternoon heat);
and when I was sad or ill she would stalk up to me and caress my
cheek with her paw. When I was at University, and she knew that
death was coming, she took herself into the drain at the bottom
of our front garden. Twice, Dad managed to climb down there
and bring her back, but the third time she went missing was the

last. Dad found her dead, with some garbage already over her. A rat ran away when he lifted the grill of the drain.

With the new house came a new school: I was to go now to Corinda State Primary School, which was on Cliveden Avenue. I entered Grade Six again, and went into Mr. Nick Bolcas's class about halfway through the school year. It was about this time that I realized that my life had been divided into two, and I was not so sure that I liked it. I remembered enough of what was bad in London, yet Brisbane seemed to be so very far away from everything; it was as though time itself was slowed down by the tacky heat, and all one could do was register the strangeness of the place—snakes that would slide out of the open pipe near the letter box, paw paw trees in the garden with withered fruit plopped beneath them, those peculiar birds you could never see whose calls were brightly colored loops and wild scribbles in the blue sky of early morning, and cicadas persistently droning in patches of bush—and wonder if it would subside after a while. I reacted by becoming far more attached to England than I had ever been in London. I wrote endless pale blue aerogrammes to Kevin and Eddie and my grandparents and devoured the London papers that were always several weeks late by the time they finally arrived. I drew the Union Jack on all my exercise books at school, wore a jumper even on warm days, and formed the firm resolution to return to London as soon as high school was over and done with.

Little by little, though, my resistance wore down, and by the end of the year I was exploring the bush near where I lived. In the summer holidays I wandered around the blond western suburbs where new houses were going up, seeking out the bush, and especially the forbidden area around Monier Road and the Private Road, the latter protected by a high mesh fence with barbed wire at the top, which reminded me of Eastbrookland but only because it had an air of danger. Others had broken that fence before I found the gap. I felt the rigor of the heat. "You do not belong here," the place would say to me every so often as I paused in a drench of sunlight, taking a drink from my canteen. "I want to," I said inside. "But you never will," it said back.

I am here, in the tall yellow grass on a slope not far from the concrete factory, making my way to Oldfield Road, but life is elsewhere, though I have no idea where. It is a cold thought on a burning day.

——— ▾ ———

Was I still on the hill Difficulty? I felt I was, probably somewhere around the bottom, but I also realized that the hill had changed many of its contours. I had been trying to orient myself in this new country with only limited success. I found my way around all right, though mostly in terms I had brought with me from London, and unlike London the whole city seemed painted on the surface of time. True enough, there were older parts of the city around Roma Street, Central, and the Valley, but they just seemed seedy, and when I walked around there with Mum and Dad the whole place smelled of stale beer. When Grade Seven started, with Mr. Peters as my teacher, we did some history. Mostly, we pondered Australian history but every once in a while Mr. Peters would get het up about something else. He seemed to subscribe to the Good Man/Bad Man theory of history. Sir Winston Churchill was a good man, for example, and so was Sir Robert Menzies, but Mao Tse-Tung was a bad man, a *very* bad man. All the hard-working Chinese had left for Taiwan, we were told. We learned Australian history in two ways: by memorizing bush ballads and by way of a new subject that I liked at first, "Maps." I think I managed to get down the first few stanzas of Banjo Patterson's "The Man from Snowy River" and some of "The Geebung Polo Club," and I found John O'Brien's "Said Hanrahan" very funny and was touched by it. "Maps" required more work, though. We had a blank exercise book, and had to buy two plastic templates, one of Australia and one of Queensland. Each Friday afternoon we traced one or the other into our book and had to do a map of some historical event.

So I made maps of where sheep were farmed and where cattle were raised and once, for homework, a map of the two; a map of Queensland showing where sugar cane grew; and a map of the States and Territories with their capital cities. We touched on history when following Captain Cook's passage up the Queensland coast, when tracking the gold rushes, and, more obsessively, when tracing the paths of the great explorers, both over Australia and particularly in Queensland. I plotted Sturt's three expeditions, around the Macquarie River, down the Murrumbidgee River, and finally his quest for the inland sea: he got as far as the Simpson Desert and fell too ill to continue. He tried again, and failed again. Another long silent Friday afternoon, the air thick and wet, was devoted to tracing the journey of Burke and Wills from Melbourne to the Gulf of Carpentaria, and one week for homework we had to map where Leichhardt most likely disappeared. We had to mark the place of all deaths with a little cross. Always, great attention had to be given to shading in the different deserts—light yellow, dark yellow, pink, red—all done carefully by drawing on blotting paper and then gently rubbing with it to make the colors smooth and even, and to writing the places named by explorers in a perfect copybook hand. Map homework always spilled over a long afternoon into the evening. Marks were given for neatness more than for content, and some girls, it was said, spent the entire weekend doing their map for homework. We were arranged from top of the class to bottom of the class, with the top kids—a little phalanx of neat girls, each formidably armed with a large tin of wickedly sharpened Derwent colored pencils—sitting in the left-hand back corner, and

Corinda School Grade 7

the weaker kids in the front row. I was in the front, on the right-hand side.

Sometimes the landscape seemed marked by the sheer resistance of the country to its white population: Lake Disappointment, Mount Despair, Mount Hopeless. . . I had heard of the Aborigines, and had seen a couple up in the Valley, dozing on a pavement with a bottle in a brown paper bag between them. Mum had crossed the street when she saw them up ahead. The only times that Aboriginal people were mentioned was when they had co-operated with explorers or hindered them or killed them. (In those days no one thought to point out that some suburbs, Goodna being one of them, had aboriginal names.) History was to do with white men, just as it was in England, the difference being that here it had been going on only for about two hundred years. One Sunday afternoon when I showed my history homework to Dad, for him to initial, he said, "'istory? Nah, this ain't 'istory, son. Nothin' but sheep an' cows so far as I can see."

——— ▼ ———

Stranger than "Maps" by far was what my teacher at Goodna had darkly forecast but which came only at Corinda. "Copy Book" looked, for all intents and purposes, like a music book for composition, yet there were not just empty staves inside, for one line had, already printed, a simple sentence written in a sloping, looping cursive with serifs; some of the letters seemed extravagant, the up-stroke on the *p*, for example, looked as though it started life with the ambition of intersecting with the moon but gave up after a brave initial effort. An entire afternoon each week was devoted to copying the exemplary script on the staves beneath, and try as I might I found myself incapable of even approximating it. Even when I improved my copybook looked a mess, since I kept sweating on it; in summer, the classroom was always steaming, despite the stilts. I knew italic script from England, even though I couldn't reproduce it, but this hand lacked its elegance, and seemed fussy and artificial; and why on earth should everyone have the same style of handwriting, especially one that seemed so lacy and old-fashioned? Mr. Peters had a special black board with staves on it and took pains to reproduce the official Queensland script. It was impressive in the way that drinking a glass of water in 317 equal sips would be impressive.

Perhaps even more useless was mental arithmetic, which was practiced religiously first thing every morning after reciting the "Our Father." These exercises consisted of working out sums without pen or paper, things like: Multiply 2 roods, 7 yards, 5 feet by 8. (Don't ask me to do it, even now.) The words "chains," "rods," "roods," "perches," "poles," and so on were no more than spots dancing before my eyes, and since I had never learned the times table, I generally got zero out of ten for mental arithmetic. One day a boy in the middle of the class asked why we had to learn all these measurements. Mr. Peters said, softly and reflectively, "Some of you one day will be farming out west and will need to calculate the size of paddocks in your station, and you won't have pencil and paper with you out in the woolshed!" (He had spent some years shearing out west himself and used to regale us with stories about how the only thing to eat out there was lamb, which you had to eat hot and cold, with sauce and mustard, anything to vary the flavor. He also told us of blokes reading Lord Tennyson around a campfire in the evening. The shearers loved "The Lady of Shalott," it seems.) By then, I had lost all interest in living out west; it was even hotter than in Brisbane, I'd learned, and even the Romance of "UNEXPLORED" had faded: parts of Oxley might as well be so marked, I'd discovered on the weekends. Besides, why couldn't you do the calculation with pencil and paper before you left the homestead or when you got back?

I proposed the objection that I would *never* be managing a station or shearing sheep, which took Mr. Peters by surprise, since I didn't speak up in class. His dark look at me suggested that I might as well have offered that we hand over the whole of Queensland to Communist China and throw in some additional bananas and a pineapple for good luck, but since he didn't dignify my remark with a response, I ventured to add, drawing on something I'd read in the local paper, that decimalization was to be introduced soon for all weights and measurements—decimal currency had already started on February 14, 1966—and then no one, not even someone standing beside the woolshed in the hammering heat on distant stations, would have to know anything about roods, perches, and chains. I didn't quite know what meters and kilometers were, but I guessed it had to be easier than all this talk of rods and roods. In any case, Mr. Peters didn't feel moved to question me narrowly. His brown eyes speared me. "You sit down here, son, right in *front* of me, so I can keep my eye on you," he said, slowly and distinctly. I could feel the sharp edges of his words. And so I got my books, pencil box, papers, and ruler, and moved into the center of the row closest to him.

I had been fortunate. Once Mr. Peters had got so angry with a boy that he called him to the front of the class and belted him hard over his knee. It took all of thirty seconds, but we were all shaken by his fury, and when he had stopped, and the white-faced boy got back to his seat, it was clear that the most overcome one in the room was Mr. Peters. He had lost control, hadn't sent the boy to the Headmaster, who was the one who usually dispensed corporal punishment, and was now most likely worried about what we would tell our parents when we got home, especially what the boy he had humiliated in front of the class would say and what his father might do. He handed out our Readers and said we could all read a story for half an hour, and he left the room. He returned with what looked like a shoebox of Wrigley's spearmint gum, and handed us each a pack, with a big smile. "All friends?" he asked, beaming. We chewed away, happy enough, even the boy he had beaten. "Why don't you all go out early for lunch?" he added, as if he were the very soul of kindness. I went to the milk shop over the road, which usually had a long queue in front of it, and bought an apple charlotte to have after my sandwiches.

As at Goodna, the Headmaster took it upon himself to come into class unannounced and talk with us about whatever was on his mind. One day an Indian boy joined us, which must have tweaked the Headmaster's curiosity. He came in during second period, stood before us, looking more or less like Mr. Heber. I had wondered before about the resemblance, and had imagined that somewhere in the Head Office of the Queensland Education Department there was a mold for Headmasters; they could be produced almost at will to supply any school in the State: they would be kept in a back room, making up problems about chains and perches, until they were old and withered, then, when needed, would be dressed in a cheap black suit, given a tight crew-cut, and then shipped out to Gympie, Bunderberg, Chinchilla, or Corinda. Or maybe teachers applied from all over the State to become Headmasters but only those who looked like Mr. Heber were ever chosen. "Sorry, Mr. Smith," a QED official would say, sadly shaking his head, and looking over his glasses, "you're a bit overweight, wear brown trousers, and have a side-part in your hair. Best you remain a classroom teacher in Winton."

However, our Headmaster had been chosen, and he was now here before us. He asked, "How would you describe the taste of *bacon*?" Silence. (Long-term Corinda students must have had experience of this sort of impromptu visit.) "How about you, boy?" the Headmaster said to the new kid. "Bacon," he said, in nicely articulated English, "is *delicious*." The Headmaster paced back and forth for a while. "*No*, boy," he said, suddenly turning on a pin, "Bacon is *tasty*!" Undeterred, the new boy added, "In my country, when we had bacon, my father always said that it was *delicious*." This was too much! No one ever contradicted the Headmaster! "What do *Indians* know about *bacon*?" he yelled. "Pigs are *unclean* where *you* come from!" He stormed out of the room.

—— ▼ ——

For all of its foreignness, primary school in Brisbane was not as frightening as attending Thomas Arnold and Eastbrook. There were teachers who were gentle—Mr. Barry Bliss who sometimes taught drawing at Corinda was like a large, soft teddy bear— though most blew up every now and then, acted eccentrically, and got in foul moods. Yet that, I had long come to recognize, was something all adults did. Something must happen to you when you turned twenty-one or thirty or maybe thirty-five.

Life must have cracks in it. Schoolwork was easier in Brisbane, though I still remained in the front row, just under Mr. Peters' watchful eyes; but the main difference between education in London and Brisbane was that the latter was slowed down by heat and humidity. By afternoon, we were all subsisting in a torpor that wasn't far from sleep, and sometimes we were simply told to put our heads down on the desk and sleep for a few minutes.

In my second Brisbane summer there was a heat wave that lasted for a few days. By the third day, the classroom was rank. We all had a little afternoon sleep, and when we woke, still heavy, the Headmaster was in the room, standing with Mr. Peters beside the thermometer. There was consultation, then the Headmaster went to his office; and then he came back and had a word with Mr. Peters at the door to the classroom. The gluey air must have been well over a hundred and twenty, and given the worried look on the Headmaster's face my guess would be that it was a great deal higher than that. It was two o'clock, and we were told to pack our ports and go home. We were too sweaty, too tired, and too cranky to be elated at missing a whole hour and a half of school, and we dispersed languidly. Some of us walked together, not talking much, past Hopetoun, which always gave me the creeps, down Cliveden Avenue, past Morcom Avenue, and into the little park just off Ardoyne Road where we looked in vain for a tap. The light was quivering. About halfway through the park, which seemed never to end, the scene before me went grainy. I woke up minutes later, shaking my head, and saw two other boys still on the ground. A lady in a long frock from one of the houses was running towards us with a cup and some water in a plastic bucket. Did we ever need it! "Get on home now, boys!" she said. I picked up my hat and dragged myself up Seventeen Mile Rocks Road, turned into Brittain Street, and, after a tall glass of icy water, collapsed on my bed.

———— ▼ ————

Mum took a sewing job up in the Valley, and was out of the house five days a week, working with young Italian girls. At morning tea they shared the *cannoli* and *sfogliatelle* they made at home and brought to work, and Mum would wax lyrical about it all when she got home. She seemed younger than I had ever seen her. She liked the girls so much she brought a giggle of them home one Saturday when Dad had to be at work. They came in the late morning with baskets of food and drink, and immediately took over the kitchen, putting on colored aprons they'd brought with them, assigning one another tasks and repeatedly saying, "Sitta *down*, Rosa; *we're* making the *pranzo!*" They were to make ravioli from scratch. I went to my room to do homework, but it was difficult to concentrate because of the ribbons of laughter in the kitchen; eventually, I was called for lunch. Everyone had a bowl of ravioli with meat sauce except for me, for my plate had just the one large cushion of ravioli. "Whoever gets the *raviolo* has to do the washing up!" one of the girls brightly said, giving me a hug. "I think I'll have some of the little ones," I said, joking, though that is what I had wanted all along. The ones in the Heinz can were like that. "*Ma va' là!*"one cried. But in concert they gaily extolled the virtues of the *raviolo*, and I knew Mum wanted to enjoy herself with her friends. She even had some red wine, which was the first time she had ever tasted any. It was the one and only time I saw her utterly happy.

Already she was working hard, in the city and at home in the evenings, and before long she quit her job in the city in order to work only at home, going into the city only to buy cloth and thread and buttons at a store. Sometimes she would take me and I would marvel at the pneumatic tube system that zipped above my head, each little brass cylinder making a soft landing on the desk just before the customer with the correct amount of change. For her, though, no more *zeppole*, no more *bombolonas!*

And not so much giddy happiness, either. Things had changed in another way as well. When girls came to be measured, fitted or to collect, I was relegated to my bedroom or the kitchen. Mum had already seen how I looked at girls when we were shopping in Oxley, and those looks exiled me from the little world of the living room. I had already managed to stay in that room for months longer than I had any right to.

Pauline, too, found a job. There was no call for anyone who could speak French or German in Brisbane, unless you were a teacher, and so she got a clerical position in Myer's on Queen Street in the city. Only once was she asked to help out when a Frenchwoman *sans anglais* came into the department store, wanted to buy some clothes, and couldn't be understood by anyone. Soon enough, one of the supervisors in the store took an interest in her; and one hot Saturday afternoon a car drew up outside our house, and Charlie Vella, wearing shorts, a stripy shirt, and a vast grin, revealing a gold tooth, got out. Mum saw him at the gate, and Pauline gasped and ran into her room to make herself presentable. Charlie announced that he was taking her to the beach, so she changed again.

Soon that "Vella fella," as Mum called him, was often around to pick up Pauline or deliver her back home. One Saturday he took me along with Pauline on a day trip to Mount Tamborine, miles inland from the Gold Coast. I sat in the back of the car, and almost immediately my shirt got stuck to the back seat. "Not summer till the steering wheel's too hot to touch!" Charlie said, and drove off. We had a picnic and I knew enough to make myself scarce for a couple of hours. So I followed a rainforest bushwalk to see Witches Falls; it was supposed to take no more than an hour, and I was a fast walker. After an hour and a half, with no Falls anywhere to be seen, I realized that I had taken a wrong turn somewhere, or probably more than one wrong turn. I was lost in the bush again, and the rainforest was denser, more outlandish, and more dangerous than any I had tried before. There were branches that had fallen here and there, and every so often a crack above me made me jerk straight up. I thought I could find my way back by recalling figs that seemed as if they had melted in the intense sunlight and cycads that were like small explosions of fronds, but there were more of both than I had thought, and I was now walking uphill in the late afternoon, the sun breaking through the trees now and then and heavy on my head. There seemed to be no air on the mountain, and for a while I had to sit down on a mossy log and figure out what would happen if I didn't find a way back to the car. That was becoming increasingly likely, since every way I turned the forest looked exactly the same. The only thing I could trust, I came to see, was the gradient: I had been walking down when I started, and now I was walking up. I emerged from the forest, thirsty and tired, and came across Pauline and Charlie entwined some distance from the car. Later that evening, in my bath at home, I noticed little marks on my stomach. "Dad!" I called urgently, "*Dad!*" "Dunno wot *they* are," he said, darkly, and walked off to ask the man next door who was always fiddling about in his garage on the weekends while his wife sat behind mosquito netting inside. They were ticks, and they had to be burned off me with an extinguished match that was still hot.

—— ▼ ——

One thing that is impossible to convey in these pages is the mental and emotional fog in which I lived both in London and my years at Goodna and Corinda State Schools. Sometime in my early childhood I had retreated into myself, to a place where I could not be threatened, and so thoroughly had I withdrawn there that I could hardly be enticed out. In London I went about with friends, though I mostly lived an inner life when with them, surfacing only every so often, like a train coming out of a long tunnel before disappearing into another. In Brisbane I found it harder to make friends: I was subsisting at the bottom of the class, morbidly shy around adults and bigger boys, fearful of the future, drawn to girls, and did all that I could to avoid PE, swimming, and sports. We had swimming classes each Tuesday morning, but knowing that you were automatically excused if you had a cut I would cut myself just above the level of my short pants with Mum's German cutting-out scissors and put a band-aid over it before heading off to school. I would sit in the classroom by myself with one of the Readers, or would test my memory of one of the bush ballads that we had to learn by heart, but mostly I would just look out of the window and let time go by.

I spent my free time either in my bedroom reading comics, tunelessly strumming a badly tuned guitar, or, more often, wandering by myself around the bush nearby. One of my favorite places to go on a Saturday afternoon was up over Seventeen Mile Rocks Road and into the Oxley High School grounds, from which I climbed a steep track of red clay like a vein running into thick bush. There I could be more fully alone. The Brisbane River looped around there, and I could sit on a fallen gum and watch branches make their slow progress in the great brown river down towards Ipswich. Late one afternoon a large black snake pulsed straight past me; my blood froze, and my body knew to edge backwards into the bush. My mind idled on those adventures, without the fear that it couldn't engage the tasks we were given at school. My report cards were missives of sorrow received with resignation. I regularly failed mathematics, got nowhere at all in mental arithmetic, was hopeless at "Copy Book," messy with "Maps," had no idea of grammar, was quite unable to draw, wrote stories set on weird planets or in the age of the dinosaurs that Mr. Peters couldn't make head or tail of, and of course absented myself at PE and sports as often as I could. It was always possible to sit on the toilet for half an hour. I could memorize bush ballads and repeat them oddly with a London accent, but that talent wasn't assessed or reported. Mr. Peters's comment on my term card was invariably, "Kevin should see me before and after school." Mum packed me off to school earlier from then on, but I waited on the corner of Cliveden Avenue, near Hopetoun, so as to get to class just as the bell was ringing, and I made a dash for the door as soon as the bell rang in the afternoon. The thought of spending time alone with Mr. Peters upstairs in that classroom gave me the willies.

An inner life was all I had; it was at once all-consuming and never more than a mist. I received intense, amorphous stimuli from the bush, and from what I saw of and around Brisbane. The Botanical Gardens, Lone Pine Koala Sanctuary, Mount Tamborine, the ferry to Dunwich, along with stretches of wasteland and bush, and also girls seen walking down the street or looking in shops: they were all passively absorbed, but all that haunting overripe richness seemed to go nowhere. I was just taking up space and time. Nothing of my solitude ventured out of me, and the future was not going to put up with me for much longer.

——— ▼ ———

Towards the end of year seven at Corinda one of the girls, another Pam, held a birthday party at her house one Saturday night. It was the closest thing to a grownup party that any of us had been to on our own account, and we apprehensively looked forward to it but with little or no idea of what to expect. It was a warm evening, and when we arrived it turned out to be a BBQ: Pam's father was cooking sausages and burgers and onions outside, the smell curling round and about the entire street and making a few passers-by, on their way out for a walk, pause for a moment or two to take it in. There was a girl who had left our class at the start of the year but who had now returned for the party. In truth, it was hard to recognize her, for she seemed to have grown up three years in six months, and now looked like a slightly younger version of the girls who frequented our living room in the evenings. She tried to teach us how to do a simple dance that she had learned somewhere in her bright new world, which she beautifully exhibited to all of us, though only a couple of the girls managed the steps. The garden started to blossom with music from a record player, and there was a little embarrassed dancing. I could tell that my partner, a girl a few desks away, had put on perfume for the occasion. One or two others were wearing lipstick, probably for the first time. But then Pam's father declared that dinner was ready and we were to queue up for a burger.

"Onions?" he asked. "Yes, please!" I said. But a boy just behind me whispered in my ear, "No! What if we play 'Spin the Bottle'? They'll be on your breath!" I declined the onions. "No point in wasting good fried onions," the father said, and I regretted seeing them scraped away. It hadn't occurred to me that this would be a party where we would pair off, and as it happened it wasn't. All the girls there were in my class, and, unlike Goodna, there were no tactile glances silkily going back and forth between boys and girls, or certainly not going from boys to girls. Pam, though, slipped round the back of her house into the bushes with a boy from another school she had invited, which released little bubbles of whispers among the girls who remained. "Come on back, Pam," one of them shouted after a while. "You must've kissed him long enough by now!" So she returned, holding his hand, and brought with her the vague sense that the reason for the party was the very event we had just witnessed. The dancing between couples gradually fell away, and almost all of us went back to playing games, just as we might have done after school if the girls and boys had played together. We had stepped up to the line of adolescence, peered over it, and then retreated to being twelve. At least we boys had, more or less.

The smell of jasmine thrilled the garden; it became difficult to tell who was who in the dark, and some kids were slowly departing without being seen. What could one say, after all? Pam's parents had withdrawn into the house, and she was dancing barefoot, slowly and closely, with her boy by a fire that had been lit outside. A machine for zapping mozzies was snapping and cracking, and cigarette smoke wafted from an open window in the house. The moon was full, or nearly so, on my way home; and in the sweaty moonlight I could see people in their hot, dark rooms crouched before a smoldering TV, and when I turned into Brittain Street I passed a house with the back door open and only a fly wire screen separating their lives from mine. There were voices saying something or other about a baby, but through them I could hear Glen Campbell singing "By the Time I get to Phoenix." And I remembered that young girl running and crying so hard through the park in Southend a couple of years before.

5 ▸

There were two related surprises in my last weeks of primary school. First it was announced that a final summation of our schoolwork, going back over several years, would be undertaken by our teacher to see if we could progress to high school. This came completely out of left field, since I had assumed that all of us would be going to Oxley or Corinda High as a matter of course; only one or two of the girls had quietly let it be known that they might be attending Brisbane Girls or Somerville House. For those of us who sat in the front row, forever under Mr. Peters's steely gaze, this was disturbing news, or so I thought. I talked with the boys on either side of me, and it turned out that they wanted to take on apprenticeships in any case. Then came the second revelation. There was to be an athletics test to see who could advance to high school. This was too much. No one had said anything at all about this to us before! It looked as if my future was to be decided all too soon. Maybe I could get into a culinary arts school somewhere in Brisbane; that wouldn't be too bad. In fact, on reflection, it might be infinitely better than going to Oxley where I would have to learn logarithms. (I had seen a book of them, owned by the willowy girl, two grades ahead of me, who lived over the road, and I thought it had to be learned by heart.) It would be more interesting to throw myself into making *crème brûlée*, *tarte tatin*, and *flaugnarde*, none of which could be made in our hot little kitchen, and all of which looked seductively at me from the photographs that I had seen of them. Besides, I rather fancied myself in one of those bouncing white chef hats.

The athletics test was the first of the two things suddenly thrown before me. On the appointed day a chesty PE teacher sent by the Government was already hard at work while we steadily dripped into school. There he was in the middle of the oval putting up ropes, marking running lanes with white paint on a roller, and setting up the long jump. He must have been there for hours. There would be sprints and laps of the oval, other kids had divined from the pattern of ropes and paintwork, as well as high jumps, long jumps, hurdles, and relays. They were excited—no schoolwork! But for me the field was beginning to assume the aspect of a final, grim Judgment. We all changed into PE gear and went out to assembly. I could feel my future tightening around me. By now there was a female PE teacher, with legs like the trunks of stinging trees, standing beside Chesty; and inevitably the girls went one way and we boys the other. Our beefy fellow in shorts and loose armless shirt quickly arranged us into groups for the sprints and runs; our names were already typed on his clipboard. "Now boys," he began in a nasal voice rather thinner and higher than I had expected, "we're going to be out here all day, and no one will be leaving until we're all done." (Pause while he scanned our faces for the slightest flinch.) "I've got all your names here," he said, patting his clipboard, "and everyone has to do each exercise and receive a mark for it." (There was another pause while he surveyed his morning's work on the field.) "Any boy who doesn't pass today's test," he said, now speaking very deliberately, "will have to repeat year seven." (He paused to let the information sink in, then smiled.) My escape route to culinary school had suddenly been blocked. There was nowhere to go but straight ahead.

Chesty hammered a post into the ground, and we were to line up behind it when not in any race. "There," he said, when he had given the post the last thump, and, pointing to the field on which we were all standing, added, "that'll keep it down all day!" We tittered out of politeness or nerves or, in my case, both, and soon enough we started in earnest. I sprinted as fast as I could, and did better than I could ever have imagined, a result of long legs and fear; I did less well in the relay, since I dropped the baton when it was being handed to me; and I ran out of puff in the long run around the oval, but came in just as Chesty's stopwatch was about to stop. I could hardly see for all the sweat in my eyes. The sun was now working hard. Hurdles were another matter entirely. I threw myself at the first one with as much gusto as I could muster, raising my right foot, I thought, to somewhere near my stomach, but knocked the hurdle over, and clattered down with it. In the process of staggering up, I upset another hurdle to my right, belonging to the parallel race for another group of boys, and so caused a halt to the entire event. I could see Chesty making an annotation on his clipboard. "Hart, Kevin: Hurdles, o." Or "Hart, Kevin: Moron."

I limped over to Mr. Bliss who was on duty as the First Aid Officer, and who was surveying the whole proceedings with a faint sense of alarm. He always had the air of a man facing a world hiding something vaguely threatening just behind the distant scenery. Sometimes, when surprised, his eyebrows were like an acute accent and a grave accent. He was the only teacher who did not like to be called "Sir," but I could never think in advance to make an exception for him. "Sir, I just hurt myself in the hurdles." "*Please* don't call me 'Sir'! Just 'Mr. Bliss' or nothing." "Yes, sir." (Much rolling of the eyes and an infinitely long sigh.) He told me to return to the school and to sit down for a while; and this withdrawal, which I dragged out for as long as I could, saved me from the high jump and the long jump, each of which would have been fatal to my future, even if I had not hurt my leg. From the safety of the benches near the taps, I saw Mr. Bliss talking with Chesty, and I bet he was saying that I'd have to be evaluated on what I had already done, since it would be dangerous for me to continue if I had already hurt myself. So: Hart, Kevin 1; Chesty 0. And so the day ended, and I faltered home, inglorious but victorious.

At dinner I told Mum and Dad what had been said about not being allowed to go to high school if we didn't pass the athletics test, and I also let out that there was to be a grand report on our primary school years that would be taken into account as well, and that if you didn't pass you had to repeat the year. "You'd better go to see the Headmaster, Jim," Mum said quietly, not looking at me. "Can't 'ave Kevin repeatin' Grade Seven; he's already a year older than the others." So Dad dropped into the school in the early afternoon a couple of days later; he must have arranged an early shift at Sergeant's Factory that day. I saw him walk along the corridor, looking lost, as he usually did when out of his usual ellipse of life, centered in family and work, but he wasn't around when the bell rang. What had transpired between Dad and the Headmaster? What wisdom did that grave Authority with the ruthless crew cut dispense? When I got home, I was told that I would be going to Oxley State High. There were no entry tests! The athletics afternoon had no bearing on getting into year eight, and there was no final report on one's entire career in primary school. Those were just stories that the teachers had made up to scare us, Dad said. I had no idea what had been said in the Headmaster's Office, but Dad was none too pleased at what he had learned. I think he must have got shirty with the Headmaster. Hart, James Henry 1; Authority 0. The world was indeed changing.

————▼————

The summer before year eight seemed to last forever; afternoons would bulge with time, and sometimes all I could do in the syrupy heat was lie on my bed and try to read something; and as evening came on the scent of the garden palpitated with the jasmine, jacarandas, and frangipani. I could stand on the back porch and see wave on wave of fruit bats flying overhead, many going to Indooroopilly Island in the Brisbane River, but not for very long; clouds of mozzies would quickly come. Week after week my bedroom also had the rich dark smell of fresh leather and the gluey tang of many new books. The leather was my briefcase, bought specially for high school, and the new books were in piles all over my room. I had to cover them in plastic myself before the first day, which I did so assiduously Mum found me one night at my desk cutting plastic wrap in my sleep. From time to time, I would open a book and look inside; apart from the ones for English—a collection of essays, some novels, and an anthology of poetry—they all seemed unintelligible, especially the mathematics and science books, but the freshness of the ink and the intoxicating scent of the paper and binding more than overcame that apprehension. Everything said, "New Life!" I had been told that, if things didn't work out, I could leave at the end of year eight and try out for culinary school. The year seven report that I had received from Mr. Peters was very far from encouraging: I was third from the bottom of the class and, as he noted, had never bothered to see him before or after school. I wished I could have given *him* a report card. "Mr. Peters is a lazy sod, given to bouts of violence; he's smarmy, and was probably a lousy shearer. And since he has a mustache, he'll never become a Headmaster!"

Finally, though, I was free of primary school; and soon enough I might be free of the whole wretched business of school! It was a liberating thought, and oddly made me feel happy to be walking to Oxley State High School for the first day. It was only a short way, a cut through two gardens, and then down a winding path into the gully where the buildings were clustered, hidden from traffic zooming up Seventeen Mile Rocks Road to Jindalee. It was a new school, clean and without character, and the bush had been devastated to make it. But I could plainly see the vein of red clay leading up the hill, and I knew that river on the other side and the pleasures of sitting beside it doing nothing apart from watching it go by. Waiting by the stairs to "A" Block, I caught up with a couple of boys from Corinda, and met some other boys I'd run into on weekends who had come from Oxley State Primary.

I had been to primary school, high school, and then primary school again and then once more, and now I was back in high school. Once again, I was walking from class to class, and only the novelty of the place, the new faces, and the uniform, hid from me that most classes were just a blur. I was still in the phase of identifying myself as English through and through. I clung to my accent, my prize possession, and all my school books, along with my homework book, had a Union Jack on them, and in my inner life I was still in London, albeit a London cleansed of the shadows that I had known all too well. I would be a chef there one day, perhaps in one of those fancy restaurants in the city or in the West End that I read about in the fat papers that still came heavily in the post each month. At lunchtime I would hang around with other boys from England, most of them still in the camp at Wacol. Several had families that were just biding their time before returning home; in turn, they were marking time at school. We talked of the first division, who got relegated and who hadn't, and then passed to the latest in British pop music and the sorts of guitars that were being played these days: Contessa, Fender, Gibson, Norma. . .

Two classes that weren't a blur were Woodwork and Metalwork, and that was only because my complete lack of talent in them made them stand out for me and made me stand out in them. Unlike other subjects, everyone could *see* just how bad I was; my joints and seals were awful. I knew from Eastbrook that

I hadn't inherited anything from my grandfather in the way of carpentry, and now I could imagine him gazing at me from London with flecks of grave disappointment in his eyes. These were classes for those boys who were going to leave after year eight and take up apprenticeships, or after year ten and enter a technical school. The teachers were men who had actually worked for years in trade, and they had a separate block of classrooms and their own staff room. Their Australian accents were far more broadly pronounced than the other teachers, with whom they seldom mixed, and they used idioms that I hadn't heard, or heard in their voices, so much so that sometimes I couldn't understand what was being said. "Get out the road!" the woodwork teacher, Mr. Dittman, shouted out to me when he was trying to get past me with an armful of sawn-off planks, and I was awkwardly chiseling away at an innocent piece of larch. I walked outside the classroom and stood in the road, thinking that I must have done something gravely wrong. But what was it? "What you doing out *here?*" he asked, exasperated, a few minutes later when he'd noticed I wasn't in class. "You said for me to get out into the road," I said. "No I *didn't!*" (Look of incredulity.) "Now come back in and get back to work!" He sat down, dabbed his forehead, and then went for a tour of duty around the workshop, which, thankfully, did not include me. My cheeseboard was already looking as though no self-respecting block of cheddar would ever associate with it. My sanding of the surface made a big dip in the center, and the rest was far from smooth. Cheese and splinters anyone?

I wanted to shift to Home Economics, which was scheduled against both Woodwork and Metalwork, but despite my parents' tepid efforts I was kept in the "manual classes." The Deputy Headmaster, Mr. Trevor Dyer, gave the distinct impression it would be like letting a fox into a chicken coop. He had short black hair pressed down with Brylcreem, so that it looked as though his hair were painted on his head; and since the remorse-less Queensland sun didn't agree with him, his face and neck were always treated with face powder. He squinted when he looked at you, and would bring his face close to yours; it felt as though he might be inspecting the state of your soul and finding it sadly wanting. My ardent wish to do Home Economics because I wanted to go to culinary arts school was met with blank incom-prehension, much as if I had indicated that, on leaving school, I would choose to wear panties and a bra, and I was pointed back to the "manual classes" with the sage advice that I would find my experience there very useful one day. (That day has yet to come.)

——— ▼ ———

Dad mustn't have been doing so well, since he had to go to the local doctor, something he would put off for as long as he could. He had stopped being a "postie" and now worked at Ser-geant's, a metal shop in Sherwood, where he assisted the fitters and turners and metalworkers with their work. Faced with the doctor in his white coat and a stethoscope dangling round his neck, surrounded by medical instruments and books, he must have become inarticulate. He told Mum that he just couldn't tell the doctor what was the matter with him, though he indicated to her it was to do with his "waterworks," a word he probably self-censored in the surgery. It all came out as *wotsits, thingamies, thingamabobs, you-know-wots,* and *wot d'you-call-its.* He became embarrassed and had to leave. But not before the doctor did the usual tests: weight, heartbeat, pulse, temperature, and blood pressure. The last of those was morbidly high: 220 / 115. "Mr. Hart, you should be *dead!*" the doctor had said, looking him straight in the eye, he told Mum. He must have been forty-eight or forty-nine, and it wasn't the first time this had happened. Even though he had landed safely in Brisbane, and now had a decent job, he worried about everything. Would the house ever be paid off? Would there always be work for him at Sergeant's? What would happen to Kevin? Had they done the right thing in coming all this way? And now he was worried about his health. He was given some pills to help and told to have a holiday. "Easy for 'im to say. 'ow can we afford *that*?" he complained to Mum.

Slowly, he started to relax a little more; there were no more graveyard shifts, as there had been at Beckton, and he and Mum slept in on the weekends, making good use of a Teasmade that they had bought. It sat on a bedside table, next to Dad's dentures, a jar of Steradent, and a glass of water. Since my bedroom was just opposite theirs, I could sometimes hear them making love early on weekends. (Once I accidentally disturbed them when they were quietly at it: "Look at 'is face, Jim!" Mum erupted in laughter, while Dad was busy on top of her. In a hurry to get out, I slammed their bedroom door and rushed into the shower and then, soon as I was done, out the front door.) He used to read in London; now he didn't: a large futuristic TV dominated the living room, and soon there was a smaller one in their bedroom as well. A radio was never turned off in the kitchen. Somehow this constant chatter must have reassured my mother, making up for the buzz of conversation she had enjoyed when working in town with those Italian girls, though it made doing homework harder for me than it already was.

"Don't shut your door!" Mum would crossly shout out if I attempted such a thing. This was clearly a hanging offence, since who knows what a thirteen-year-old boy would do behind closed doors. Curiously, she wasn't at all worried that I wanted nothing more than to wear an apron and do all the cooking on the weekend. With my pocket money I bought gadgets to chop vegetables and mix batter, and I brooded over the few cookbooks that we had. Somehow that could all be done while spending time roaming around the bush, watching *Kommotion*, with its go-go girls, on Saturday mornings, or even Julius Sumner Miller on *Why Is it So?* late on weekday afternoons. I didn't understand the physics, but I wished that I had a crazy science teacher like him. Doubtless these things reassured my parents that I was "improving," but in truth I was living the same inner life that was as much a mist to me as it had always been. The difference was that school was more benign; at long last, there was no need to fear being thumped by anyone.

——— ▼ ———

Someone high up in the Queensland Education Department must have read Plato's *Apology* at University and misunderstood the sublime expression, "The unexamined life is not worth living." For life in Oxley State High was a constant ripple of examinations: weekly tests, half-term tests, term examinations, and other tests thrown in for good measure, like those sent to the school from that inscrutable organization the ACER. I imagined that this outfit had floors of glassy offices somewhere in Canberra with solid English chaps perpetually composing new tests. "Now Jones," one of the senior men would say at a meeting, "how about you work out a good old test on recognition of colored chalk." "Yes sir, sterling idea." "Strange to say" (looking thoughtful), "there's been no really thorough analysis of whether all children can see yellow chalk as well as they can pink chalk." "Quite so, sir. Don't worry, I'll have something on your desk by the end of the week!" "Good man. Carry on."

In my first half-term test I remained true to form, gaining dismal results. The little blue booklets came back to me covered in red, with a predictable "See me!" written on the cover with an impressively low grade firmly circled. You could almost hear the teacher's sigh as the circle of ink was made. I was not so very concerned, since I could leave at the end of the year, and I could get through each day without being buffeted by the chill winds of education or bullied by the older boys, and, once home, I could withdraw to my bedroom or play with Sooty or Peppi or settle down before the TV. I didn't go to see any of the teachers before school, at lunchtime, or after school. I talked with boys from the camp about West Ham, Tottenham Hotspur, or Manchester United instead. At home I assiduously kept a cardboard League Ladder more or less up to date by reading the London papers.

The first term examinations were looming, and after them would come report cards, and teachers had to hurry to complete all that was to be taught. In mathematics this meant that we had to be introduced to algebra, and quickly too. I remember the first class as if there were a framed photograph of it on the mantel piece that I can see each day: I was sitting in the middle of the room, about the exact center of the row, and the teacher wrote a simple equation on the board: $3x = x^2$. Perhaps the principle in play had not been satisfactorily explained before the equation was written on the board, for there was a murmur of panic that fluttered through the class. "Huh?" one girl a couple of rows behind me said. I could hear another girl leaning over to her friend and whispering in a breathy voice, "If it's three lots of x, how can it be equal to x squared? It can only be equal to itself." Another bright girl wondered aloud how something that would be a line could be equal to something that was a shape. For most of the class, though, what was written on the board might as well have been in Sanskrit.

The odd thing is that these questions were precisely the kinds of thing that had always come into my mind, had stood there as obstacles blocking the door, and could never be surmounted; but today they didn't. Instead, something else happened. I suddenly felt as though my mind was moving; it was exactly as if there were a dirty window long since rusted into place that now, for an unknown reason, was being dragged open with tremendous force. Disoriented, I must have looked as though I was not paying attention, but in truth I was. I had never had this experience before. "Are you drifting off again, Hart?" the teacher asked, in a weary voice. "No, Miss." "Then can you tell me the value of x?" I heard myself say, "Three," to the surprise of most of the kids in the room, as well as the teacher, and, more strangely, to myself as well. "Who else gets that?" Miss asked. Two or three hands stiffly went up. Then, looking at me with a mixture of indulgence and curiosity, Miss asked: "And *how* did you get the answer?" Again, I heard myself say, "I divided both sides by x." My explanation came after seeing the right answer, and that was nothing if not peculiar. "B-u-t how do you know what x is to begin with?" one of the girls at the back blurted out. "You don't," Miss said, "you have to find out what it is." And the lesson continued, and I understood it all.

I went home and looked at the mathematics textbook, and before dinner I had gone through the remaining chapters on algebra for the term. Sometimes I didn't even need pen and paper in order to do the problems; I certainly didn't have to go treading in that boggy center of the times table. Algebra hardly ever required anything beyond the three times table. I had the strange sense that my mind had been opened: I could see the world about me so much more clearly. A couple of times, just sitting there in my bedroom, familiar objects burned with intensity when I glanced at them. I said nothing to my parents at dinner about what had happened. Quite simply, I couldn't say anything because what had occurred at school and then in my bedroom made no sense to me. I felt, though, that I had been helped over a line that I had not been able to see, and now I was definitely on the other side of it. But would it last? On which side of the line would I be when I woke up tomorrow? I went to bed unsure who I was now or who I would be the following morning.

Over the next few days at school I found that I no longer had difficulties with any of the academic subjects. Science suddenly seemed easy, especially once I checked the textbook, and I found that I grasped French grammar, which was coming thick and fast as the end of term raced towards us, without any trouble. Vocabulary had not been hard to learn, but I had drooped when tenses were in the air. I became eager for the school day to finish so that I could go home, do my homework, which now didn't take long at all, and then go back over what I was supposed to have been learning since the first day of school. One afternoon I reviewed all the science that we had been taught, and read ahead a couple of chapters. Why had I found it so unintelligible before? By the time the term examinations came I had studied all that we had been taught, and the tests didn't seem hard at all. The blue booklets were returned, and the teachers' comments all had the air of complete and utter surprise. "Well done!!!" was written on one booklet, "Huge improvement!!!!" on another. (We had been told in English that exclamation marks were to be used sparingly, and we should imagine that we were given only a hundred of them at birth to last us all our lives. Now I was causing teachers to use up their allotment for most of the decade on my first-term examinations.) "What had happened?" a couple of them asked me when we passed in the corridor. That was my question, too. (Yet a dark thought lurked in the back of my mind: Would it last?) When report cards came, I was first or second in all the academic subjects, though near the bottom of the class in Woodwork and Metalwork. Only the fact that I could read a rule and the tidiness of my bench saved me from being right at the bottom.

I took home the report card, and left it on the arm of Dad's armchair, and then went to take Peppi for a long walk down Oxley Station Road, Englefield Road, Douglas Street, and home again. He was very happy; I was euphoric. Yet when I got home Dad was not at all pleased. He was looking intensely at the report card. "'ave you made this up?" he asked gruffly. "No!" I said, taken aback. He took the card over to Mum, who was sewing, and said, "'ere, Rose, 'av a look at this!" She did, and it was as though time stopped for a few moments. Her face didn't move. "Can't be right, can it!" Dad said, with that lost look coming over him. "Don't be daft, Jim. Look at the numerals; no changes there, an' this ain't anythin' like Kevin's writin'. You done well, boy!" (beaming). "Dunno, then," he said gloomily, "Can't be right." There was an injured silence that night at home, and the next day Dad phoned the office at school. Yes, he was told, the grades were indeed as written. "Sorry about the wot-d'ya-call-it last night," he said, "just couldn't believe it." He looked lost again, and although I was still wounded, I also understood why he would act he as did. "See how badly I did in Woodwork and Metalwork," I said, in a bizarre attempt to make him feel better. "No use to you, son," he said, with an embarrassed smile. "Never was any good at 'em myself. It's your mother who knows 'ow to make things. Got that from yer Granddad."

—— ▾ ——

My classmates took my academic transformation in stride with hardly a raised eyebrow. Not so the teachers, especially those who oversaw the school. They alerted the Faculty of Education at the University of Queensland to the oddity they had discovered, and the response was entirely predictable: another battery of tests. This time it was a series of IQ tests, which I had to do while in class with a lesson humming around me, and kids glancing round at me. I did them without much enthusiasm at the back of the room, and then, a few weeks later, I was called up to the Headmaster's room. "A man from the University has come to see you," his secretary said, and pointed me into a room; it had a desk, two chairs, and a slim tweedy man in an orange shirt and brown tie sitting in one of them. Mostly this man seemed concerned with what I wanted to do when I left school, and when I told him that I had been thinking of leaving at the end of the year and going to a culinary arts school he was caught completely off-guard. He looked at me as if I could not be serious, or as if I was engaging in a special sort of game with him (which itself could possibly be of interest, his face suggested), and deflected my answer by reminding me that the academic path in school was doing mathematics and science, and I should dedicate myself to that. I had a gift for mathematics, he said, and I owed it to myself to develop it. I left the room, pleased to have heard what he said and also pleased to be out of his gaze; I felt I was a curiosity for him.

I knew what he meant, though, since I had long imagined the man I would become, and to whom I owed all sorts of things; otherwise, he would not exist. The trouble was that now I was being pointed to another man I would become. I had still been able to keep the original one in sight, as if just a block away, since I could always return to England and being a cook somewhere in London was something he could do. But how could I owe something to a man I could not even picture? Besides, I hadn't borrowed anything from him in the first place. The closest I could see to such a person was the Lecturer in Education on the other side of the table, and I wasn't all that sure that I wanted to be like him. He was a type I'd never seen before, and I saw a weakness in his eyes that his patter couldn't cover. So I returned to class where all eyes were on me for a moment or two, until the teacher told us we were moving on to the next chapter of our text. I smiled at Libby, a girl I liked a lot, and took my place, and the world regained its balance.

On one of my irregular trips into the city on a Saturday morning, where I had used to wander around, mainly just watching girls, I visited the Queensland Book Depot, and went immediately to the mathematics section. There were books on algebra there, including one on algebraic geometry. I couldn't afford any of them, but I worked on some Saturday mornings washing cars in a garage on Oxley Station Road and saved up my pocket money, and finally was able to buy all of them, including one I hadn't seen on the shelf before that quickly became my favorite, G. H. Hardy's *A Course of Pure Mathematics*. I made my way through the books on algebra easily enough, though the hardback volume on algebraic geometry was far more difficult: I was at sea with the notation, and the proofs were overly compressed for anyone anywhere near my level. I persisted with the thick tome, however, mainly by seeking to master more algebraic geometry than would ever be taught to me at school. Was I giving my older self what I owed him? I didn't know, but whole Sundays slid past me while I sat still, pursuing geometry and algebra with Sooty asleep by my feet under my desk. It was as though I would best be able to capture the problem, and bring it home (somewhere in my mind), only if I were completely still and quiet. Then I would pounce, and it would be mine. Suddenly, though, I would look up from my book and the paper covered with diagrams and x's and y's, and realize that I hadn't eaten since breakfast and the smell of dinner cooking on the stove was wrapping itself around me. Within a few short weeks I had taken steps over that border I had been made to cross, and the horizon before me kept withdrawing so that I never even started to come close to it. Somewhere behind that horizon was the person I was supposed to become.

——▼——

My life had already been divided into two, England and Australia, and now it had been divided again, this time far more surely, between my time before the algebra class and time thereafter. My ambition had not changed, however: I still wanted to become a chef, and I still wanted to leave school, even though it now posed no threat to me at all. I did not understand what had happened to me, and doubtless because of that had apprehensions that my change was accidental and temporary. I would wake up tomorrow, the day after, or the next month and find that I was back in the mental fog in which I had been lost for nearly all of my life. I did not know quite what to think of that possibility, since I was enjoying being able to grasp concepts and read all sorts of books, and was exploring the intellectual world I had found so forbidding as quickly as I could; and yet, at the same time, I could remember that the fog was comfortable. I could retreat into it at will, and now I felt as if I was standing in a well-lit field. Now and then people would come by to prod me and see how I would react.

Who was standing there, though? The first dividing line had yielded someone who was now sentimentally English, which didn't make any sense at all because he had hated so much of his time growing up there; the romps through Eastbrookland and afternoons rambling around Folkestone, were just occasional glints of light in Dark-Land. And what about the second dividing line? It was impossible to say, for in many respects I was no longer the same boy; I had been inverted, put firmly on my feet for once, and also saw the world in sharp relief. My mind was like a stomach that had never been fed, and it demanded continual offerings. There simply were not enough hours in the day to appease it. At night it seemed to work overtime as well: there were always dreams so florid, so rich, and so elusive that when I woke up, I was shaken by them at first and then troubled that they had escaped me. I felt at once overfull and as though I had a leak in my mind.

Yet not everything about me had changed. Far more confident in schoolwork, I was still timid in class, and, moreover, still lived most intensely within myself. Sometimes it felt as though my outer life was a cleverly organized illusion, a projection of about five percent of myself into the alien world of space and time. I had emerged from another Dark-Land, a landscape where intellect was no more than a distant lighthouse, submerged in deep fog, the pulse of which could be discerned only vaguely, intermittently, and sometimes hardly at all. I was quietly investing in yet another country, in which I could live without fear while bathing in the warm light of understanding. Was I climbing the Hill of Difficulty? Or was it changing its contours again, giving me the sense of ascending it, while all the time I was simply walking into another Dark-Land? Those questions did not come into focus for a long time.

They were not the most urgent questions I had to ask. I could sense others moving around inside me, in my mind and in my flesh, twisting and turning, kicking, pinching, and nipping me. They never came into view or stayed still, and at times, like tapeworms, they sapped my energy, even hugely recharged as it was by new knowledge and a zest for more. For homework one evening my English teacher, John McGrath, required us to learn a poem by heart: Shelley's "Ozymandias." The assignment was easy; the poem went directly into my memory after no more than two or three silent readings, and there it started a job of work, releasing—or perhaps creating—emotions that I had never had before, or at least had never wanted to prolong. Now I found myself savoring them. As I quietly recited the sonnet to myself, alone in my bedroom, the final line and a half started to stand out, as when one turns over a page in a fold-out book: "boundless and bare / The lone and level sands stretch far away." What was responsible for the melancholy that suffused my whole being as those words formed in my mouth and met my ears? I looked and looked. It was the play of the *b*'s, the *l*'s, the *s*'s, and also the open vowels, but how could the movements of those sounds produce a feeling that was at once intolerable and desirable?

I had read other poems at school, including the bush ballads, which, except for "Said Hanrahan," had had little or no effect upon me, and over the coming days I went back and re-read the poems we had read in class, usually without much discussion of them. "Attack" by Siegfried Sassoon, which had been roneo-ed in smudgy purple ink and given out to us, did not move me as Shelley's poem had done, though the opening lines of a short sixteenth-century lyric surely did: "Westron wynde, when wilt thou blow, / The small raine down can raine." I had read those lines a week or two before the algebra class, and they had hardly brushed me as they went past, but now the second line was like an electric shock. The adjective "small" had something to do with the effect, as did the repetition of the word "raine," but nothing I could see in the line could explain or even make clear the nature and the power of what I was feeling while saying it to myself. It would be years later before the lyric as a whole released its full strength, for in the school anthology I had the final lines read, "Cryst, if my love were in my armes / Or I in my bedde again!" The disjunction turned down the charge of the poem to somewhere close to zero. Only in the first year of University, when I was studying English and had a proper anthology, did the poem flash before me: "Cryst, if my love were in my armes / And I in my bedde again!" The greatness of a poem can turn on the most ordinary word in the language being in the right place, and, luckily, it can also triumph over the prudery of censors.

—— ▼ ——

I started reading more poems and began writing them as well. At first, it was easy enough to find poetry that mattered: I had an anthology, and could borrow books from the school library and from the Corinda Public Library, both of which had small collections, which was all that I needed. I walked to Corinda one afternoon after school and checked out a volume of Shelley's poems, and lay on my bed in the late afternoons and read

several of the poems over and over to myself. They blocked out
the radio and the TV. I had hoped for more sonnets like "Ozymandias" and found much that washed over me, like "Queen
Mab" and "Epipsychidion"; yet "Ode to the West Wind" gripped
me far more than the sonnet had done, and I tried to persuade
myself that I liked the last lines as well but could never do so in
good conscience. I had become a critic, albeit a very reluctant
one, since I didn't want Shelley, this man I fiercely loved, to have
weak moments. A couple of years later I would buy a little red
volume of his poems at the Queensland Book Depot and again
would ponder many of them, fearing the end of "Ode to the West
Wind" each time I read the poem because I knew it would disap-
point me, and this time being drawn above all to "The Triumph
of Life," less to what was said, which I couldn't always make out,
but to the magnificent roll of the verse right up to "Then, what is
life? I cried." It was a richness of line that attracted me in those
poems, and it would be several years before I weighed Keats's
advice to Shelley, "load every rift of your subject with ore," and
understood its justice in others of his poems.

I do not know whether it was my memories of the scraps of
English countryside I had seen or stirrings of religious desire, or
both, that had me gravitate to Hopkins. When I read "The Wind-
hover" the first time I was thrilled, and I still am each time I re-
read it. In bed each night I would read the Penguin paperback of
his poems that I had bought in town, and would sometimes fall
asleep with it in my hands. Mum would come by on her way to
bed and remove the book from me and put it on the side table
where I would pick it up on regaining consciousness. Hopkins's
Victorian England was hardly Eastbrookland, however, and
my experience of London was not his, either. It was inevitable
that, when I came upon it, I would resonate with Eliot's grimy
London—its street lamps, gutters, smells of chestnuts, showers, chimney pots, and all—and I read his early poems intensely

without losing any passion for Hopkins. One poet quickly led to another, and before long I was a hardened and shameless reader of modern English poetry. Only later would I be introduced to modern Australian poetry, first Judith Wright and then Kenneth Slessor. The memory of reciting Banjo Patterson in that sweaty classroom in Corinda had blocked any interest in Australian poetry at the time.

I ranged further afield than the Queensland Book Depot and made pilgrimages to the American Book Store on Edward Street and the Red and Black Bookshop in Elizabeth Arcade. Between one and the other place, I found slim volumes of modern American poetry, and also a volume by Miroslav Holub in the Penguin Modern European Poets series. I suppose that the anarchist owner of the Red and Black Bookshop believed that contemporary American poetry, along with poetry written behind the Iron Curtain, would lend fuel to any revolutionary spark in his customers. Later, I would buy books on anarchism and socialism, and I subscribed to *Anarchy*, which would discreetly come each month from England. Yet in grade eight my sole focus was those slim, inexpensive volumes of verse. I started to collect the Penguin series—volumes by Apollinaire, Prévert, Quasimodo, Rilke, and others—and over the months and years ahead hungrily looked for other Penguin anthologies on the shelves, such as *The Penguin Book of Japanese Verse*, *The Penguin Book of Sick Verse*, and *Contemporary American Poetry*.

Those thin books, along with the more substantial anthologies I had, were slowly forming the vanishing points of my life, and the projection that started to appear between them was none other than the world of the poems I was starting to write. They gleamed with more passion than skill. Shelley, Hopkins, Eliot, Yeats, Hardy, Cummings, Williams, Thomas—the list grew wildly, and without shape—had become my teachers. It was as if my education had suddenly flexed: I was one student with a whole classroom full of teachers. And if they were dead that fact changed nothing at all, since they seemed far more alive than anyone I knew, including myself. Once again, I was being divided: now it was between mathematics and poetry. My parents never came to terms with the change I had undergone in the preceding months, though they figured it in just one way. I had become adept at mathematics; the fermenting of language, poetry, was something secondary and potentially dangerous because it could easily be a distraction. Now that I had "turned a corner," as Mum said, I could do just as the gentleman from the University had said, and take the hard science and mathematics track. We were told about the choice we would have to make in the third term. Classes were rigidly stratified into 9A1, 9A2, 9A3, 9B1, 9B2, 9B3, 9C1, 9C2, and 9C3. The C group was for girls who would be leaving school after grade ten and seeking commercial work. ("By the time you get down to 9C3," one boy joked, "the chairs are brighter than the girls sitting on them!" I didn't laugh: I used to take Peppi for an evening walk, circling and circling one block in particular, so I could dawdle outside the house of one of those girls going into 9C3 in the hope that she might be walking barefoot in her garden as I went past and I could stop, surprised to see her, and casually talk with her.) The B group was for boys, also most likely leaving at the end of year ten, to undertake technical work of some kind. The A group was academic, and it was inevitable that I would go into that stream. It had always been certain, for my stark inability at Woodwork and Metalwork put the B stream out of the question. The only choice was which subjects to take, Science or Arts?

One day one of the senior teachers came in to give us some advice which way to jump. "It's easy to work this out, boys," he said (ignoring all the girls in the class), "if you're smart you do science, if you're dumb you do arts." I wanted to take arts and mathematics, French and German, and I also wanted to learn how to type, but the combination proved impossible. For a start, only the girls in 9C could do the typing class. Either you took Mathematics A and B and Science A and B or you took Mathematics A, Science A, Art and History. And you couldn't take two languages. Since I would be taking English in any case, and I was already tuned to French, I chose to fill out my schedule with double Mathematics and double Science. So I went into 9A1. My parents and teachers were relieved, and I knew full well that if I had leaned in the other direction I would have found my arm being twisted behind my back by all concerned.

It had become apparent shortly after my first term record card that attitudes towards me had changed. Teachers now took an interest in me, and would look at the book I was carrying around and ask what I was reading. At school that book was always one or another volume of mathematics, usually G. H. Hardy, since I kept poetry mostly to myself. Only my English teacher knew about this other passion, though even he had no inkling just how fiery it had become. At home, though, things were different.

———▼———

Dad never understood the sudden transformation of his son. *One day the boy was almost at the bottom of 'is class in everythin', causin' untold worry as to 'ow 'e would get on in life, an' then the next day 'e was at the top of the class in just about everythin'. One day 'e was wanderin' 'round the bush on the weekends, doin' God knows wot, with nothin' passin' through that mind of 'is; the next 'e was sittin' at 'is desk with a heavy volume propped open before 'im, fillin' page after page of notebooks with squiggles and drawins of I dunno wot. One 'oliday before startin' year nine 'e took a stack of books to the beach, an' instead of runnin' around on the beach with ovver kids 'is own age wrote wot 'e thought was a better introduction to "differential calculus," wotever that is, than the ones he had been readin'. 'e 'ad never learned 'is times table, but, so 'is teacher said when I went to see*

'im at the school one night, knew far more maths than all the teachers
at the school put together. 'e just didn't know wot to do with 'im, that
teacher said, an' 'e wondered wot would 'appen if 'e kept learnin' at
this rate. 'e would be very bored at school; 'e already was, 'e thought,
and wot good would that do? Maybe 'e could be promoted early an'
do 'is wotsits and go early to Uni. But would that be any good for 'im,
even if 'e stayed in school for a couple more years? Even then, 'e'd only
be fifteen, too young to go off by 'imself! Dad was still fretting.

Yet our relationship didn't change in the slightest; we were
always close, without having to say much to one another. Not so
with Mum. I had been raised in the warm intimate life of mea-
suring, fitting, and collecting, and then lost it once my interest
in girls had started to manifest itself, and when that warmth vanished all that replaced it on her part was a mixture of indifference and anxiety. By then, Mum had given up any hope of me
finishing high school, and was resigned to me going to culinary
school. Also, she was scared stiff that soon I would be "chasing
after girls," as she put it, and before long I was doing just that,
or, rather, a slower, more soulful version of it, filtered through
poetry. She had always contrasted Pauline and me and always
to my sister's benefit—she was bright, outgoing, and confident—and I couldn't help but notice that as soon as my grades
shot up she turned the full beam of her attention on me. Pauline had married; it was not going well (her husband would end
up serving time); and she had fallen from the heights of youth.
When her husband was behind bars, she returned to live with
our parents and she returned to being a teenage daughter under
her mother's thumb. She brought a big dog, Vicki, with her, and
a white fluffy cat, Penny. Sooty would go prowling around the
house, looking for Penny who, unbeknownst, had climbed onto
a shelf and would hurl herself down on Sooty. At night, both cats
and both dogs slept on my bed. If I turned over, there was an
explosion of growling and hissing for a minute and then a warm

resettling. I would wake, feeling like Gulliver pinned down by the Lilliputians.

Mum would silently come up behind me when I was working at my desk of an afternoon, and look over my shoulder. I could smell the soap she used, mixed with sweat, and hear first her thongs flapping and then her heavy breathing on my neck. She'd read what I was writing, or look at the little pile of *Anarchy*'s I had, or at the strange symbols flying across the page, and then walk off. Sensing her creep up behind me, through that door that always had to remain open, with the TV and radio nattering away, I would cramp up, or sullenly put down my pen, or stalk out into the garden. It was always worse if I was reading or writing poetry; I had no privacy at all, and I covered what I was doing, just as I had learned to do at Goodna. She had plans for me to take lessons playing golf. "You make contacts on the golf course," she said, knowingly, as though disclosing one of those secrets of adult life, doubtless imagining her slow son now a doctor playing with other doctors at the Brisbane Golf Club, and getting referrals on the basis of a good swing. "There won't *be* golf after the revolution," Chairman Hart said. "Oh, *don't* say fings like that!" she wailed. "You'll get into *trouble*!" And she walked off, thongs flapping loudly.

Despite my far-left politics, which my parents hoped were only a temporary madness, I had magically become the better option in the family for bearing the next generation and any little Harts it would produce into middle class respectability, and I could see right away that the reward for that was display after display of affection, especially before the neighbors. "I want you to be a doctor or a lawyer," she said one day when we had to decide which path to take through high school. I had been in a doctor's rooms many times, in London and Brisbane, and had no desire to be the man in the white coat. I remembered all too clearly one winter's evening when I was eight having to wait outside in the days when the river froze while the queue to see the doctor slowly shortened. I had a terrible flu, which had been bothering me for a couple of weeks, and now my ears were bleeding. We were outside on the road, then, after a while, inside the surgery, and then, after a wait, we got a seat, and finally, an hour later, saw an exhausted doctor for a few minutes. I felt an immense relief when we left and stepped out in the biting night. I'd rather be sick, I thought, than at the doctor's. Dad wrapped a scarf about my ears, I put on woolen gloves and plunged my hands deep into my coat pockets, and we walked home. To be a doctor meant an endless queue of sick people, crying babies in an overheated room, chemical smells, urine samples, and dirty bodies. It was far better to be a chef. I had no idea what lawyers actually did, but I was brought up to live in fear of the Authorities, especially anything to do with the Law; and no number of report cards could wipe that away. What had happened? My sudden change at school at first released me into a new world, an inner sanctuary of light and feeling, and now it threatened to become an instrument to take all that away from me. Dark-Land had many guises, it seems, and there were all sorts of hidden paths that could twist and turn and take me back there.

When I won a scholarship for years eleven and twelve a couple of years later, Mum wanted me to use the money to board at "Churchie," a C. of E. grammar school in East Brisbane. The very idea filled me with horror, and I felt betrayed. I had escaped the bleak world of education, more or less. At Oxley I had friends, including a Dutch girlfriend, Irene, who was so pretty I had to keep an eye on her, and had been largely left to my own devices. Schoolwork was easy, and once it was done I had time to read and write and dream. I certainly had no wish in the big wide world to enter a grim castle of rugger and rowing, trumped-up house spirit, bullying, and what the books and magazines I had been reading taught me to call petit bourgeois life. My political principles had started to form, baggy and immature yet strongly felt, and they were violently opposed to the direction in which I was now being pointed. Besides, by then I could finally discern the way out; my long abandoned attempt to run away from home had shifted gear and become a waiting game. At the end of year twelve it was natural to leave home and go somewhere else. I had imagined after that first report card that my longing to leave would be mitigated by satisfaction at school, but instead things at home had got worse.

I flinched before my mother's newfound displays of affection for me, her continual hints that somehow she was responsible for the transformation I had undergone. Had she forgotten what she had said, only the year before, about me being an accident? At first numb, and then living with an open wound that simply would not heal, I had been unable to do anything to dissipate my anger; it had been sublimated by mathematics and poetry and, as I started to see, a patient one-sided game with my mother of keeping quiet and letting time pass. I was also letting air out of any room in which we were together. Nothing of importance was ever articulated at home; any attempt at conversation about relationships and feelings was regarded as rudeness and ingratitude. I tried it one time, never again. To leave would mean being away from Dad, but I knew that I had to get away, and the sooner the better. My academic success had become a sort of weapon.

———▼———

I was also being pulled by another force that frightened my mother in particular. As a child, my religious longings had been only vaguely and very partially satisfied by hearing John Bunyan and by reading small passages from the King James Version of the Bible. Sometime well after the first algebra class, those cravings, as they had become, burst like a weakly fitted hose that is simply blown apart by internal pressure. A new boy, Philip

Schalchlin, from Arkansas had joined my class at school, and his father was a pastor of a missionary church set up in the hall of the Country Women's Association near Oxley Station. He invited me to the Youth Club that they held at their house on Friday nights. I went; their house was grubby, and there were food stains and footprints on the worn sofa. His mother was fat and waddled around barefoot. Outside, where we went to play tag, their garden was just dirt and weeds. Yet there were some sweet girls in the group. I started attending their church. There was nothing wrong with going to church according to my parents, as long as it was the Church of England, although, for my mother, nothing much good would come of doing so, either. The Church of England was a venerable institution that did no damage, even if clergymen had a talent for sticking their noses into other people's business. Probably God would do that as well, I imagined my mother thinking, or maybe she thought he was too well brought up for that.

The Southern Baptists were unlike what I knew of the C. of E. in almost every way, except in their use of the King James Version of the Bible. Their hymns were passionate and melancholy. The pastor's wife or his bobbysocks daughter would play the piano, and there would be drawling southern voices crooning away at "Are you Washed in the Blood?" (with sidelong glances at those who were perhaps insufficiently bathed in that vital fluid), "Jesus is Calling" (at once lonesome and tender, as though singing a lullaby), "Bringing in the Sheaves" (with gusto, in case the Second Coming occurred that very night and one might be judged wanting in fervor), and that old heartbreaker "Just as I Am," always reserved for last, to entice people to step forward and give themselves to Jesus. The sermon was the main attraction, though, and it would last an hour or longer. Invariably, it would converge on the Book of Revelation or the Book of Daniel. In that hot room, with a portrait of the Queen at the front, with mozzies flying in through the open door and windows, with empty freight trains grumbling past on the way to Ipswich and, from there, to Toowoomba, Charleville, and way out west, the hymns finally ceased; we had been raised to a high enough level to receive the Word. Starting slowly, the preacher would work himself up into a sweat. It would pour down his face; it would make his white shirt stick to his flesh; it would hang on the dark curling hairs on his arms. Always, he would begin with a passage of Scripture, and we would follow along with our own Bibles; and often he'd seize the Bible from the podium and wave it wildly as he got into his most intricate rhetorical coils from which there was no escape, either for him or for us.

The miraculous, the celestial, the demonic, and grisly forebodings of what was going to happen (and soon), flared before us, Sunday after Sunday. One evening the text was taken from Matthew 12. It was read with conviction and devotion in equal measure. For this was the truth, much as it would be if reported in *The Australian*, but in the black book he held before him, which he could navigate blindfolded, truth was bigger than anything we would ever hear today, it included the supernatural and would not stay bound within covers; it leaped out of the days and weeks of our small lives to touch the grandeur and terror of the last day. He started:

Then was brought unto him one possessed with a devil, blind, and dumb: and he healed him, insomuch that the blind and dumb both spake and saw. And all the people were amazed, and said, Is not this the son of David? But when the Pharisees heard *it*, they said, This *fellow* doth not cast out devils, but by Beelzebub the prince of the devils.

Everything in the man's face and voice declared that this was a true event, and that had people back then had cameras and tape recorders they could have caught on film a devil leaving a man or a woman. Beelzebub was every inch as real as David and Jesus and those Pharisees, maybe taller than them or maybe shorter. Had you been in the Holy Land that day, you would have seen Jesus raise his hand, you would have heard a scream, and then you would have seen the man's entire body relax. A demon would appear, you'd see his tormented face, and then it would vanish, like a poisonous vapor. How could you not believe?

He broke off, looked around the hall, taking in each face, each one of us potentially damned for all eternity, wiped his forehead with a vast white handkerchief, and continued, his voice now rising, his forehead straining with effort to stop the tremor that started to undulate through the words he read:

> And Jesus knew their thoughts, and said unto them, Every kingdom divided against itself is brought to desolation; and every city or house divided against itself shall not stand: And if Satan cast out Satan, he is divided against himself; how shall then his kingdom stand? And if I by Beelzebub cast out devils, by whom do your children cast *them* out? therefore they shall be your judges.

He had started to tremble, both in his voice and in his body. That huge man, well over six foot, probably once a quarterback on an Arkansas high school team and now running to fat from too much fried chicken, mashed potato, and gravy, quavered under the pressure of Scripture as it cascaded from his mouth. Would he be equal to preach about this sacred moment? Jesus was watching him, he knew, but could he do justice, even a weak human form of justice, to the words with which he was

entrusted? Was *his* congregation divided against itself? He
continued:

> But if I cast out devils by the Spirit of God, then the
> kingdom of God is come unto you. Or else how can one
> enter into a strong man's house, and spoil his goods,
> except he first bind the strong man? and then he will
> spoil his house. He that is not with me is against me;
> and he that gathereth not with me scattereth abroad.

He stopped in order to let the terrible closing words sink into us,
and then he said them again, slowly, enjoining us to beware the
great sin of scattering abroad.

This was his theme this thick, humid evening, and it was
a tremendous one, heavy with the fat fruit of revelation. For
there were people in the church, he said, who pained him and
who pained Jesus as well, people who had not given their hearts
entirely to the Lord, who kept one foot in the world, fools as
they were, who could not see Satan when he stood before them
in the plain light of day. The clearest face of evil in our day, he
told us, was Communism, which we could see in the exploits of
the Viet Cong; and to not fight those demons was to not stand
with Jesus. America was standing with Jesus, and so was Australia. (I glowered; I was not standing with LBJ or Harold Holt, as it
happened; I thought evil had quite another face, and one much
closer to home: Vince Gair of the DLP.) But Vietnam was nothing, he said, gently putting the Bible back on the podium; it was
as nothing. For Armageddon would not be in South-East Asia, no
matter how bloody that war might become, no sir, it would be
in the Middle East, and it would dwarf any horror that we might
apprehend now in Vietnam. We could have no idea of what desolation was waiting for those who would remain on earth, not
rising up to Jesus when he appeared in the skies. He licked his

forefinger and thumb, and, following a path that the Holy Spirit had uncovered for him right then and there, quickly passed to a chapter that we had heard him quote almost each Sunday.

Safe and sure on familiar ground, he read, exultantly, from Revelation 16. No tremor now. The words thundered across the hall:

> And the sixth angel poured out his vial upon the great river Euphrates; and the water thereof was dried up, that the way of the kings of the east might be prepared.

> And I saw three unclean spirits like frogs *come* out of the mouth of the dragon, and out of the mouth of the beast, and out of the mouth of the false prophet.

> For they are the spirits of devils, working miracles, *which* go forth unto the kings of the earth and of the whole world, to gather them to the battle of that great day of God Almighty.

> Behold, I come as a thief. Blessed *is* he that watcheth, and keepeth his garments, lest he walk naked, and they see his shame.

The dragon was the Soviet Union, he explained (as he always did), and the battle of that great day would be between America and the Soviet Union; it would be played out in Israel, in the Valley of Armageddon. America stood beside Jesus, and whoever stood apart from America would be scattering abroad. They would be sent to hell after the last days where they would burn everlastingly. Their punishment would be horrific. For the damned would spend all eternity scratching a board, their nails breaking day after day, splinters going into the quick of their fingertips, and they would never be able to lift their hands from that board. Never would they be able to stop the sound of endless scratching; never would the pain diminish. Their nails would break and then grow back. No matter how often they cried to God for forgiveness God would not relent. They had had their chance. Now they must pay the price.

With that, he had reached his crescendo; he sat down again, and wiped his forehead, a button near his belt straining hard against his shirt. (Had it popped, it would have gone directly into his wife's lap, since she always sat immediately before him, and I half-wondered if she sat there in case of that very possibility.) From scattereth abroad to scratching a board: had he simply got confused, or was it intended? Before the question could take hold, there were catcalls from outside. A bunch of skinheads from Inala had been bothering the local milk bar on the corner of Cook Street, and now were lounging outside the CWA Hall, making fun of the preacher's accent and rhetoric. He tried to lure them inside so that they too could be saved; but they continued to sit outside, chewing on chiko rolls, smoking, and drinking cokes. He went to the door and pleaded with them to come in. "Jesus wants you just as you are!" he said, movingly. "Fuck Jesus!" one of them yelled from the shadows.

That preacher stepped back inside, and went back to the podium. His face was heavy and white. "I have turned the other cheek," he said, "but to no avail." (Pause with look of infinite sadness.) "I can reason with those boys once, and I can reason with them twice" (casting around the hall, with a tear forming in each eye), "but if they don't mend their ways, well, there's a place for boys like that." He gave another sermon, impromptu, on the evils of boys wandering the streets with nothing better on their minds than disturbing good Christian folk. These were boys who drank beer, he said, shaking his head, who danced with girls at parties, who caused their parents to worry. By the time he ended, no one was outside, and the milk bar had closed. When I got home, my parents were anxious. "Where've you been?" Mum asked. "Only church," I said, "It went longer tonight." "I wish you'd stay 'ome," Mum added, lighting a new cigarette. "Nothin' good'll come of it, you know," with a look of certain knowledge of the future. "'ow was it?" Dad asked, relieved and, as always, curious about it. "It was all about scratching boards," I said. "Never 'eard anythin' about scratchin' boards when I was at Sunday School, a boy back in London," he said, and rubbed his stubble. "Must be all sorts of things in the Bible I dunno," he added, with sorrow in his voice.

— ▼ —

In the August of my second year at Oxley there came the Ekka, as usual, though we had missed it each year before then. Mum and Dad and I went one afternoon, taking a special train to get to the Show Grounds. We looked at cows and sheep, pigs surrounded by their piglets, and horses and ponies brought in from farms and stations out west; there were ducks, turkeys, chickens, and roosters stepping high, to see up close, along with fluffy chicks. I was still a London boy, and this was the first time I had actually seen many of these animals, and certainly the first time I had encountered their huge smells along with soiled straw and feed. The farmers, usually wearing wide brimmed brown hats, were mostly quiet, massive blokes. Perhaps one grew bigger than city dwellers out there west of Toowoomba, with all that space and all that heat. More interesting were the dogs and cats, all being groomed for competitions, and we wondered how well Sooty and Peppi would do. If there were a competition to knock pens and pencils off a desk, I thought, Sooty would win paws down.

We moved around with the crowd, and did what the crowd did, drifting in to see the decorated cakes, which I inspected with care and sadness. Culinary school had been slowly slipping away from me in the past couple of weeks; it was going into that abyss of possibilities that are never realized in life. I could feel it losing its grip on me, and I losing my grip on it. No longer did it sit in the hard, bright circle of light before my eyes; it had become like those girls a year or two above me at school who made me go weak when they flounced past, girls I would never take to the pictures, never touch and never kiss, whose lives were always to be at a tangent to mine, who would go out with boys who had already left school, were working in shops or doing accountancy courses somewhere in the city, amassing possibilities that would become real, become life itself. For a moment, I stood there, standing in line with others for a strawberry sundae, and could see those possibilities pouring away from me at an untold rate. The young man who had studied history and art was vanishing before he had even laid the slightest claim to life, so was the one who had learned German; the bold sun bronzed fellow who went to Rennes and found Dominique, well, he had left long ago, I saw now, without even saying farewell. How could I not have seen him leave? Each day I was not becoming this person or that person; the field of life before me was narrowing, and as I slowly walked towards it, it would contain only those possibilities that were left. Was I choosing them or were they simply those that remained? I could not see them, and I wondered if they would even be there by the time I arrived.

That preacher thought that Jesus would come soon. Perhaps when he appeared in the sky only two or three people in all this giddy mass of faces would begin to rise. They would go up, slowly, to where the air is thinner and the light more intense, and meet with others from other lands who also had been plucked up in the midst of pleasure or pain. There were sure to be many Americans, if that preacher was right. But was he? I had never seen their vision of things so clearly. What if I was chosen and rose up through the clouds but beneath one of those girls at school and when I looked up to greet Jesus saw her panties instead? I supposed I would fall back down to earth with a great crash and have to live through the great tribulation. Damn! If only that old Scots woman in our street had been above me, and then I would have just seen her bloomers and nothing would have happened. No, that whole view of the world, that imperialism softened by the music of tenderness and longing, was no more than one of those possibilities flaking away from me. It had come close to me, curled around me for a time, and even entered me a little; perhaps some of it would stay there, never quite go away, perhaps it was like an inoculation, but it would never claim me. It had stood before me, waiting coyly for me to take a step forward and possess it, but I had been attracted to something near it, not to the thing itself, and had stepped aside and kept walking. I did not know it before then, but once I knew it I knew it surely and always.

We walked into a pavilion with booths that sold show bags, and Mum and Dad bought me one from Nestles and one filled with honeycomb, and they bought a couple for themselves. When we got outside, the light was thinner; a few party lights were coming on and a fresh selection of colored balloons were being blown up with helium so that they could be offered for sale. A new wave of visitors was flowing off the special train, older boys and their girls who were coming for the evening when the grounds would have a more festive, more romantic feel to them. There would be fireworks later. Some were already holding hands on their way to the wonder wheel and the carousel. A couple of girls already had huge sticks of pink fairy floss, like extravagant hairdos, and were laughing hard. We walked down an alley, each eating a burger with onions, and I stopped at a second-hand bookstall, while Mum and Dad looked at some clothes. There was little in those boxes of ragged paperbacks, but I found a soiled volume of poems by someone whose name meant nothing to me, Wallace Stevens, and I bought it for twenty-five cents. Fancy writing a poem entitled "The Emperor of Ice-Cream," I thought, the strawberry sundae still icy in my stomach, and yet I shivered in the warm evening as I read "The Snow Man" for the first time over old cardboard boxes and party lights.

Walking back to the train that would take us to the Valley and, from there, back to Oxley, we passed a store selling Bibles. "It's time Kevin 'ad a Bible of 'is own, Jim," Mum said decisively. We all went in, and I saw a trestle table darkly full with Bibles of all sizes. Some had illustrations that reminded me of the preacher's sermons. "Best get the King James, son," Dad said. And so I did: black cloth, about a foot high, the Scriptures in two columns, and little finger holds to find individual books easily. We waited on the station for the next train, and by the time it came it was almost dark. Down on the exhibition ground the animals had all been led away; the hall showing agricultural machinery had closed; and I could see some of the little stalls beginning to shut down. A train came, filled up quickly, and we were all crushed together in a carriage with young families who had difficulty carrying all the show bags they had bought. As it drew away, the fireworks began, and suddenly I wanted to return. But we were headed home, inexorably; the carriage swayed back and forth, and a boy opposite me dropped a bag and his chocolates spilled everywhere. His father, a little worse for wear, helped to pick them up. I looked into the deep honeycomb show bag where I had put my books and took them out, opening the one and then the other. On the red wooden train back to Oxley, we had a compartment to ourselves. Dad started to doze, and Mum gazed outside silently as the city sped away behind us and the river glittered. I read "Domination of Black" once, twice, and found it would not let me go.

6 ▶

In their old age my grandparents moved to Brisbane to live with Mum and Dad. My grandfather died there when I was living in Geelong, near Melbourne, and teaching at a private school. Several years before, a doctor in London had written to Mum that her father was mortally ill and that he would soon succumb to heart disease, news that she did not tell him or her mother; instead, she proposed a change of scene for them. On reaching Brisbane, he gained a new grip on life; the fresh sights and smells, those invisible strange birds with their wild swirling squeals and the paw paws dangling from trees and the brightly patterned snakes that would suddenly slide out of a drain, animated him, and he lived for several more years. It was an equivocal pleasure for my parents; they had escaped London and now, by assiduously following back road after back road, it had found them out in a distant country. It smelled of Dunhill Navy Roll. True enough, Granddad had less and less to do without a workshop, and spent his days sitting on the front verandah looking out at the railway tracks. Mum kept him supplied with chocolates, and he ate them and smoked his pipe while he read and re-read *The Courier Mail* and got browner and browner in the heavy, yellow sun. He wished he'd come out years before. Eventually bored by the local paper, by watching the freight trains that rumbled and grumbled back and forth, and by anticipating the fleshy thunder storm that imprisoned Brisbane each late afternoon in summer, he applied himself to macramé, at which he excelled, but finally undiagnosed diabetes concluded its aggressive campaign against him, and he passed away when his heart could take no more.

His death echoed like the wall of a city finally collapsing after a long siege. It was the outer wall of my city, to be sure, and I knew that it would fall one day, yet I also knew full well that Nan would not outlive him for long, and then there would be only one wall between me and death. Without her husband sitting silently beside her and smoking all the livelong day, Nan was untethered from the world. He had been her world, or the center of it, since she was a girl. She had spent her life cleaning and shopping, doing laundry with wintry water and a mangle, and cooking for him, and now his chair beside her was empty. She sat in her cane chair with a cushion on the verandah, dozed, drank cups of tea, and for the first time her habitual kindness and softness would yield to bouts of anger. So many desires must have been suppressed in her life. "Your Granddad always wanted more kiddies," she told me once when I was home for a holiday. "'Get away with yer,' I said to 'im, 'you don't brin' 'ome enuf for us to live on, let alone anovver kiddie!'" I thought of the resentment that must have been at the ground of their marriage, all that they could not talk about to each other or anyone else, for that matter. They must have made love only rarely, decades before, and it was all too possible that they had never done it after the birth of my mother.

Yet they had been as close as breath to one another. When I was staying with them in London one time, Nan leaned over and told me something. "'ere, when 'e was out in Egypt," she said, pointing to Granddad, "I saw 'im at the bottom of our bed in the middle o' the night; 'e was just standin' there lookin' at me." Granddad nodded. Now, though, bitterness and bewilderment burst from her every few days: she would sit on the verandah, looking out over that street where nothing ever happened, then quietly wander away when no one was looking, and Dad would have to walk around the Oxley shops asking if anyone had seen her. She was easy to spot; she'd seize on people on Cook Street or Oxley Station Road and start telling them about all she'd had to put up with in life. "'e wouldn't even let me 'av a new carpet!" was one of her refrains to people she accosted coming out of the bakery or the newsagent. They had no idea who she was or of whom she was talking. Sometimes she gave children money she had secreted in her apron. "'ere luv, go an' treat yourself," I imagined her saying, still kind to a fault. Her mind was wandering, too. In the end, it became too much for Mum and Dad to handle. She had to go into an old people's home, where they visited her once a week, if that.

Some years before Nan and Granddad moved to Brisbane, I had stayed with them twice in London, each time for a few weeks. It was then, when I was in my early twenties, that I got to know them and their neighbors as well. I'd see people from the banjo going about the Becontree shops when I was at a loose end, or I'd see them in the Fanshawe Tavern on the way back from walking off one of Nan's lumpy dinners, and they greeted me as though time had not passed at all. "Ain't seen you around, Kevin," one neighbor in the banjo said one day when I was gazing through the window of the bakery to see if they still sold the cheesecakes I'd had as a child. I'd left when I was eleven and now I was twenty-two, but for the woman talking with me it might as well have been that I'd been on a holiday in Devon for a fortnight. Just chatting with people was a revelation, since they had known my grandparents for decades, though mostly from a distance. Granddad kept to himself. Nothing had ever been told to me about their background, or what they did when young. I started to realize that the photograph album, large as it was, was mostly composed of gaps.

For me as a child, Nan and Granddad had always been in their living room in their council house in Amesbury Road, much as

Nan and Granddad

the Tower of London had always been on the north bank of the Thames and the Queen had always been in Buckingham Palace. They lived in a perpetual Saturday afternoon. It was inconceivable that they had ever been young, and impossible to imagine them having parents. I had seen one photograph of Nan as a girl, but even then her face was marked by care, and the earliest photograph I'd seen of Granddad showed him to be formidable. No one in my family had ever indicated the slightest interest in genealogy, unless it was of the royal family, and I had never been curious about it myself. Was Dad right to talk about there being a "Black Hart" in London in the nineteenth century, or was he just pulling my leg? There were uncles and aunts, supposedly, and cousins as well, though I could never figure out if these were real relations or just honorary titles adopted at gatherings for the sake of the children. For the most part, my family kept its back firmly turned away from anyone not immediately related to them. The only friend they had was Kitty who lived with her husband in a huge block of dilapidated flats in Bethnal Green. She never appeared in our home and we went there only the once; it was a dodgy area, Dad said. When we went up in the lift, the floor was puddled with piss and the walls were screaming out graffiti. Mum and Dad would gossip with our next-door neighbors, but they were always "Mr. and Mrs. Bray." They never got to be on first name terms, and they never took a step inside our house or we into theirs.

It never occurred to me that my grandmother was Jewish before I went back to London the second time. I'd been in America and met many Jews, and saw things in Nan I hadn't noticed before. Back in Becontree I mixed a bit more with the locals, but my grandparents' neighbors just assumed that I had always known. There were Jews everywhere in the East End, after all, especially after the late nineteenth century when so many left Russia and Poland for London. One evening I dropped in to chat with the young couple next door. (Above the kitchen door I saw, as the wife was talking, a motto, "Of all my relations sex is my favourite!") While talking about the people in the banjo and thereabouts, she included Nan among the Jews of the area. So I learned that she was Rosie Ball, born in Camberwell, and that the surname "Ball" was Jewish. I remembered Granddad complaining all those years ago about the "four by two" barber he'd run into in Ilford, and I wondered how Nan could have put up with all that from him over the decades. Or had she kept it under wraps all that time, hiding it even from herself? Perhaps it didn't mean much to her, since no one in the family had been observant, most likely for generations, or perhaps she didn't really understand what it all meant. I knew enough by then to know that if Nan was Jewish then so was Mum and so was I.

When I went to University, I had joined a Christian group that was loosely affiliated with the Methodists, but when I was in Palo Alto, California, I attended the local Anglican Church; and at the end of the year I was confirmed in San Francisco. I was still clambering up the hill I had known since childhood in London. Without knowing it at the time, I was well on my way to becoming Catholic, and when that happened a few years later, much to the chagrin of my mother, I thought I was somewhere halfway up, or thereabouts. In truth I was far closer to the bottom of the hill than to the middle of it. One thing that makes the hill deserve the name of Difficulty is that it changes shape as you walk up its paths; apparently clear ways ahead sometimes become dead ends and you must turn back, or you are led to an edge of the road that crumbles as you stand on it and you must, somehow, find another way. People have been there before you, not all of them the sort you want to be around as evening comes; so some signs have been pulled up, painted over, or turned around to face another direction, and it is all too easy to get lost if you trust in them too much. Often you are climbing upstairs in the dark. Now I had a new sign; it was in my soul—"You are Jewish"—but I couldn't make head nor tail of it.

The information sank in, but it connected with nothing else in my mind or heart. One moment in the conversation with the neighbor I had been standing in the familiar world of Protestant working-class London and the next I was, at the same time, in a completely unfamiliar world. This new world was utterly blank, since I knew no Hebrew, had never been inside a synagogue, had never had any interest in visiting Israel, and couldn't tell a *yarmulke* from a *menorah*, even if someone put the two of them squarely before my eyes. The closest I had ever been to the world of modern Jewish culture was watching a Woody Allen movie and finding it funny. I had a new identity but one without the slightest context. Then I thought: *Oh, so this is the family secret.* When I got back to Australia I asked Mum one afternoon about Nan's maiden name. Her voice went very quiet. "It was 'Balls,'" she said quickly, "an' she 'ad it changed to 'Ball.'" That was clearly the end of the conversation; I was standing on one of those crumbling edges, and had to take a careful step backwards. I simply could not imagine Nan as a girl going to Marylebone and filling in the forms needed to change her surname by Deed Poll. And Mum's shift in speech made me wonder about those days more than I had before.

The first time I visited my grandparents by myself was on the ritual Australian "grand tour" of Europe after graduating from university. I flew with a friend to London, and we traveled across Europe by bus and train, by hitching and walking. We were to go to Ireland, and I dearly wished to see Dublin, but my father was adamant that I not go. (He even took out life insurance, just in case I went. "You're not goin' anymore to that wot-d'you-call it, Ireland, are you?" he asked several years after I was back. I had no intention at the time. "Good, well I'll stop that life insurance I took out for you, then." "Life insurance?" "So we could afford your funeral," he said bluntly.) Instead of going to Ireland, I stayed with my grandparents, walked around the East End, and got to know the place much better than I had when I was a boy. I went back to the two dark schools and looked at each from the road, and I visited the Chase, which was unchanged. It was on the second visit, though, that I heard something else about my family. Dad had lost his mother a year after he was born. Her husband, William, had passed away some years before. His father seems to have been Irish and Catholic, and the story is lost under the weight of silence and innuendo. Was it a fling, a rape, or what?

If I had grown up to adulthood in the East End, I would have known that it was full of Jews and Catholics. I would have got to know Whitechapel and Spitalfields far better than I had, I would have walked along Hessel Street or High Street and seen Kosher poultry dealers and shops with boxes of Matzos in the window, or men outside little shops selling bagels in Wentworth Street. I would have got to know, just before it slipped forever into the past, a stretch of London filled with Ashkenazi Jews, more like parts of Poland than like England, and more like life in the thirties than in the sixties. I might have seen all the signs, still in the East End then, of Irish migration that had been coming on since the eighteenth century. Had I grown up there, among those Catholics and Jews, I would have learned that many sons and daughters wanted nothing more than to escape from the social stigma of being one or the other.

So my father came from Catholic stock and had married a Jewish girl, the easiest thing in the world to do in the East End after the War when people wanted new life, had closed an eye because they wanted the world to change so badly, and doubtless resented the tight-knit world of the East End with its run down streets and narrow mindedness as much as they enjoyed its familiarity and security. Or maybe he simply did not know or, if he did, didn't care that much. The War did not destroy the older generation's awareness of people's roots, though, and my grandfather quietly—and sometimes not so quietly—detested both groups to which my parents belonged, faint though that belonging was. My childhood, I started to see even more clearly than before, was composed of silences, of things withheld, passed over, rejected; it was a life of gaps, of people and events that would never be named.

I had been an introspective, slow, dreamy child, but I would have been perfectly capable of understanding more of the family's past had it been told to me. The intense focus on the four of us, huddled together in a council house as an economic unit with emotions carefully rationed, with weekly visits to Becontree, and rare meetings with ghostly distant relations, was the product of a denial of the past's power to shape us and an inarticulate urge to remake the family, if possible, for the future. Cutting all ties with England was not simply a matter of fear of unemployment; it was also prompted by a deeper, untold desire to erase any aspect of the past that could mark one and stymie an attempt to begin anew. I was part of their hope for that new life; it was the only chance I would have, they must have thought. The depth of their resigned disappointment with me, Mum's fury at my avoidance of school, started to appear concretely before me.

When Nan's mind started to wander, when she started to reveal things about the past, my parents must have been frightened about what might be accidentally thrown up in the present. On coming home for a holiday once I said I was going to see Nan in the home. "You don't 'av to do that," Mum said, tightly. "We'll all be goin' in a few days." But I wanted to go. I had loved her all my life; she was the only one who would hug me when I was a child, and now she was beginning to fray. In town I bought her a big bunch of flowers. I carried them down a long white corridor with one room after another, most with doors not quite closed. I passed a room with an open door: several old men sitting up in bed, sagging over, as if hanging from a single hinge. I stopped and saw that the man closest to the door had skin like tissue paper, torn here and there up his arm.

Nan liked the flowers, and fussed around until she found a vase for them. Then we sat and talked on her bed for an hour or so before she had to take a nap. "Wot you wanna go and see 'er for?" Dad asked roughly when I returned. "Won't do no good, you know. She's not in 'er right mind an' dunno wot she's sayin' 'alf the time." A few days later we drove up to see her. "If we get there at noon, we can 'av 'alf an 'our before she 'as to go in to dinner," Mum said at breakfast. "Then wouldn't it be better to go earlier?" I asked. She flung a look at me. The visit was carefully arranged so that we spent next to no time together. We sat on a verandah with the other old people, some slumping in their chairs, and nothing much was said. One man with a trim white mustache kept talking about nuclear war. "The world's going to end!" he kept saying and shaking his head. "I'm glad I'm not going to live much longer." He looked pointedly at me. "I wouldn't want to be your age!"

It wasn't long before Nan passed away, and then my parents had a few years together when they were at ease. Dad had retired from the XXXX brewery in Milton, where he went to work when Sergeant's closed down, bringing his working life unexpectedly full-circle, and Mum did less and less dressmaking at home and finally stopped altogether. They had worked hard, had put a little money aside, and now would have neighbors over for a BBQ in the back garden on birthdays or special occasions, or they would go over to a neighbor's for a beer or two. Mum bought an electric organ and tortured the whole street by playing simple tunes as badly as they could be played; and she took up painting by numbers. Her creativity, though, had always been in dressmaking, and that was behind her. She had to wear a neck brace now; all those decades of bending over the Singer had exacted a price. Yet she seemed content. Perhaps both of them thought that they had escaped the past, and in any case, theirs had been a happy marriage. They had survived. The secrets that they had kept from me were not dire ones, I came to think, and Mum presumably did not want them ever to be known for what she thought was a good reason; they might have injured my chances of getting into that golf club and the life of which it would have been a part. Neither of them had the faintest idea what I was really doing by way of work. I was teaching down south, something or other called Philosophy—or was it Theology? or Literature?—

and was writing poems. None of it made much sense to them, I didn't make much sense to them after year eight, although they were proud of me in a fuzzy way. I had joined another sort of club, after all. They had been right to leave and come here. It had worked out well.

──── ▼ ────

Not so long after she had retired from sewing, Mum was diagnosed with lung cancer. She had smoked since she was a girl learning the rag trade, had given up for a while because Dad kept nagging her, but had taken it up again. Pauline smoked, and when they played cards of a Saturday evening Mum found it too hard to resist. The cancer had metastasized; it was now in her liver. She was told that she should get her affairs in order. When she informed Dad in the hospital, he laughed. He had thought she had said she had "shit on the liver" and not "cancer of the liver." (He had been going deaf for some years.) When I heard the news in Melbourne, anger came before sorrow. How stupid to keep smoking all those years! (The thought came with all the self-righteousness of a convert: I had smoked a pipe myself, imitating Granddad, and had ferociously given up some time before.) I remembered how she even had a slot machine installed in the kitchen in the Oxley house and kept it full with packs of cigarettes, so that she didn't even have to go to the shops to buy any.

Our relationship had never got back on an even keel. She would read any letters I got while I was staying with them, and open my notebooks. "If you're stayin' in my 'ouse, I can do as I like!" she said once when I found her reading a letter from my girlfriend in Melbourne I'd left on my desk. She'd look over my shoulder at what I was reading or writing, and she would ask about the girls I was seeing. On the occasions she had met any of my girlfriends, when I was growing up in Brisbane, she did whatever she could to undermine the relationship. Once, after returning a book to my room, I came back into the living room to find Mum telling a girl I'd brought around that she should go out with other boys, "for experience." I came to see it was a deliberate program, and so, after a while, I cordoned off that part of my life, large as it was, and put up big signs saying "PRIVATE. KEEP OUT."

I came up to see her. Pauline had said she had a month, and that I shouldn't delay coming. I had been reluctant to visit her, and the few days I spent at home were empty and arid; too many years had passed by in silence, in avoidance, in resentment and anxiety for the distance to be bridged. She was sleeping by then on the settee in the living room, and I shared their bed with Dad. Now and then she would cry out in the night, and he would get up and see to her. I had thought that I had forgiven her for encumbering me with protestations of love, as I took it to be, only when I started to succeed in conventional ways; but the act was never complete. There was a battle of wills: she was inexorable when on her territory, and I would counter by feigning indifference and withdraw. When I looked back to see the female figure I loved, it was always Nan whose face I saw; and when she had passed away I could see my mother well enough, yet felt more of a cramp than any warmth. Leaving, I kissed her goodbye on the cheek, and she walked out onto the verandah to see me get in the cab that would take me to the airport. Once inside, I could see her leaning heavily on the rail, and the morning light glistened on her cheek; and then, just as the car started to move away, she turned sharply and went back inside. Three days later she was dead, and I was back in Brisbane.

At the very end, when the pain of approaching death erupted, she had been taken by ambulance in the early hours of the night to Canossa, a Catholic private hospital nearby on Seventeen Mile Rocks Road. Years later, visiting Dad one summer, I went to the place with neighbors over the road for a vigil Mass. I closed myself on the short drive there. Some patients were already propped up in wheelchairs when we arrived; others sat as best they could in the cheap plastic chairs. The nuns were kindly. After communion I slipped out of the chapel and walked around and around the corridors, seeing row on row of neat, clean beds, and hearing cicadas chanting outside. She would have heard them as well, I knew. I managed to get through a door into the car park but found no air there, and finally let her loss unfurl over me in wave after wave. The cicadas kept up their dry rattle in the heat. Is this how the dead speak to us, constantly, obsessively, but so that we cannot understand a word they say? They must have no more tears to cry.

———▾———

My father died on April 2, 2009, or, for me, April 1, 2009: I was in Charlottesville, and he was in Brisbane. I knew he was dying; I had lived for months inside the word "dying" and would speak with him on the phone almost every night. He had told me in his late seventies, when he was alone and didn't worry too much about death, that he was amazed to have lived so long. When he was in his late forties his blood pressure had been shockingly high. What had been going on inside him then? After Mum died he had a late blossoming; he resumed going to church, made friends at the Senior Citizen's Club, and went on train trips, flights, and coach tours with them. He started reading again, which offset his loneliness, and of course he came to Melbourne to stay and to see his two granddaughters. In the end, he lasted into his early nineties, most likely outliving all his doctors.

In his last few years he had been living with my sister, just round the corner, yet as the end approached he had to go into a nursing home. He too had started wandering around Oxley and giving money away, and he needed more attention than Pauline could give him. It was "Hopetoun," the place I used to pass five days a week in late 1965 and '66 on the way to Corinda Primary School, and even then I hastened my step just a little as I did, while wondering why no one corrected the spelling mistake on the sign. Already then, when I was twelve years old, it seemed to be one of those places always in shadow, even in broad daylight, recessed as it is from the road, looking as though it didn't quite want to disclose itself to the world.

Recently, I had visited him there with my children. "How are you, Granddad?" my elder daughter asked. "Oh, I don't like it *'ere*," he said, pulling a long face. His life had snapped back of late from a house with many ventures outside it to staying with my sister round the corner to a small single room where he had little control over his day. "The brightest man in the ward!" one of the nurses said to me. "He's always the first to give an answer in our word games." True enough, he loved crossword puzzles and Scrabble all his life, despite all those *thingamies* and *wotsits*. I kept him supplied with books in large print, mostly history books, which he loved, and when he died he was reading a life of Marie Antoinette. But the place smelled of dead food, medicine, and bleach; it exuded a feeling of hopelessness: it was a place to die, and he knew it.

Even before he got to the home, he had had two small strokes. "The end is coming," I said to myself. But he recovered from each of them, and when I came to see him in a Brisbane hospital we embraced and our joy could hardly be contained. He introduced me to the friends he had made in the ward. When he died I was in my office at the University of Virginia, preparing to teach my doctoral seminar on the early seminars of Martin Heidegger. At 1:32 pm, back from lunch and making some notes for my seminar, I felt a sudden chill that went right through my bones when I underlined the word *dying* in my notes. I knew that he had passed away. I sat in a stupor. And then the phone rang hard; it was my wife telling me what I already knew. An hour and a half went blankly over me. I walked over the lawn to teach the seminar with a visiting professor from California. I felt unmoored from the world, but I needed to be in that room with my students. I needed whatever steadiness habit could give me.

——— ▼ ———

Back in Brisbane for the funeral, I stayed in a hotel in the city, caught the Ipswich line train to Oxley, and walked straight to the Presbyterian Church where the funeral was to be held. Dad had gone to the church closest to him, the Anglican one being a few blocks further away. How different we were in that. I had anguished about the division between the Anglican Church and the Catholic Church, about the rights and wrongs of the Reformation, and had finally converted. For him, all churches were basically the same. He'd go to the local Catholic church in Corinda with me when I was home, but if not he'd go with other people in the street wherever they went, and when left alone he'd go to the Presbyterians. I think he liked the hymns they sang there. In his mid-eighties, he attended an inter-denominational class, "Who is Jesus?," but he never wanted to talk with me about what was said there. I guess I had become an Authority. I spoke at the funeral, read from the Gospel in his Bible, and then helped to carry the coffin out to the car. The coffin handle bit into my left hand. Like Granddad, Nan, and Mum, he had elected to be cremated. "Don't want all that earth over me," he had said to me one day, shaking his head. I remembered then how much he liked on holidays in England to visit cemeteries. "Lot of 'istory 'ere," he used to say, looking up from a tombstone, after squinting at its inscription. Yet they all erased themselves from history. My daughters and I have nowhere to go to visit any of them.

After the funeral, I went back with my nephew and his wife, my niece and her boyfriend to my sister's house for a while. Pauline made a pot of tea, and then, quite suddenly, said she had something to say. "The moment Mum died," she announced in an unfamiliar formal tone, "Dad said to me, 'I'm not your father.'" (If ever there was a moment to sip one's tea, I thought, this is it.) It turned out that Mum had been assaulted, forced, or raped one night by an Irish man she had been seeing when she was a girl.

Mum had made Dad swear never to tell the children as long as she was alive and now, a moment after her last breath, he could unburden himself. Yet he made Pauline promise not to tell me until he had passed away, and now she could tell me, and the others might as well know too. My childhood and early adolescence snapped into a sharper focus than ever before. I understood now the family's repugnance for Ireland, why my mother, in particular, tried so hard to prevent me from becoming Catholic, why she was so upset with Pauline all those years ago, why she was so anxious about me "chasing after girls," coming home on Saturday afternoons with love bites on my neck, and why she tried to undermine my relationships with girls whenever she could. I saw at once her having to tell Granddad and remembered her saying, from years before, how she quailed when he took off his belt and how he would lay into her. And then I remembered what Dad had said about bumping into Mum on the street and buying her a drink. What he hadn't said is that he knocked into a woman who had a little girl at home. Or maybe she was right there in a pram.

I went back into the city after a while, sat in my hotel room, and revolved all these things for an hour or two. My parents lived inside secret after secret, and they were faultless at keeping them, especially the main one. I understood now more of the pain they must have felt when Marion, the first child they conceived, died in birth, why they didn't plan on any more children, and perhaps some of the distress they experienced when their son could make so little headway in life. Why the secret was to be revealed only at the moment of each death escaped me. They would do anything to avoid speaking of feelings; and yet the knowledge was to be preserved, presented when nothing could be said, when the knowledge was hard and dry and made a hollow noise when tapped. Did they think I would be angry? Probably so; they would do anything to avoid a "scene." Yet I could not find any such emotion in me in the hotel room, only an emptiness that a long story was over, a story with so many gaps in it, so many things left unsaid and, in the end, for them, unsayable. Perhaps unveiling this legacy after their deaths was a way of explaining some of my childhood to me, for now I could weigh some of those silences, measure some of those gaps and understand some of those anxieties, and appreciate the reason behind some of those looks. And I also could see what I had already known for a very long time: my father was a good man.

I left the hotel and walked around the city and eventually found myself on William Street. There was a restaurant I could see a little way ahead; it was empty, but I went in anyway and was seated at a table. I ordered a dry martini, which finally came, which I could hardly taste, and which did not have the effect I wanted it to have. Lights were coming on in the city; by now my father would be ash, and where that ash was to be scattered was another secret—my sister's; the last one to be kept. I stretched out my legs under the table and looked out at the glittering river.

───▼───

The boy I was used to look into the future and try to find me, but I was never there for him. For many years I could hardly bear to glance in his direction; my language simply would not hook onto the blankness he carried inside him. One can grasp a concept or an image, but not a fog. I had to wait for a time when the events he lived, or underwent, would show a crack and yield somehow to language, however inadequate, that might touch what he felt and thought. When that happened, those early events rushed upon me, bursting with color and apparently intact. I had lived for years in fear of being exposed again to that blankness, as if it had retained a shapeless power that might envelop me once again. Perhaps it was stronger than the man I had become, or, worse, more attractive, more comforting, than the life I had forged. In the end, I found that the mist simply parted and let me through. Or so it seemed.

Now I look back and can see that boy plain. In the series of images that emerges, I can see him better than he could ever have seen himself, and I wonder if I saw him today, playing with other boys in the street outside my house, whether I would like him at all. He was shy yet stubborn, timid yet devious. What chiefly interests me about him is how his twelve or thirteen years seem so intense that they feel as though they occupy about half of my life, and yet that fervor was lived in a mental haze that shrouded him. I brood on the secret life he had, how he recoiled from school not only because of the violence there but also because the very institution made no sense to him, and yet, at the same time, he read books from the local library as well as encyclopedias and the Bible he had at home, and lived richly in his own dream world. Thomas Arnold was the Headmaster at Rugby for a stretch in the first part of the nineteenth century, and sought to instill in his boys a vivid Christian faith. There was none of that at the school named after the great reformer that the boy I was attended, and I doubt it would have done him much good. He was scared of this world, and did not need to be afraid of another as well. Yet Christianity was introduced to him through Bunyan and the Bible, and in his own way he stuck to it, or perhaps it would be better to say that it stuck to him. It entered his imagination so deeply that it could not be forgotten; it held him tightly and would not let him go. And it made him change as he grew up.

I look back as he grows older and see him divided not once but many times, between England and Australia, between his old life and what was to become a new one, between mathematics and poetry. He was not as good at mathematics as he had been led to believe, and when he realized that he would not be in the first rank of that field or even the second or third rank, he lost interest in it altogether. At school he came up with a theorem, promptly called it "Hart's Theorem," and sent it to the Chairman of the Department of Mathematics at the University of Queensland. A couple of weeks later a letter came for him with the proof returned. At the bottom, in small neat handwriting, was "Usually known as Euler's Theorem," and some initials. Such disappointments and further divisions of himself were not to stop in early adolescence, though he could not have known it at the time; and I cannot judge whether they honed his being to a finer point or multiplied it and rendered it diffuse. He grew up to look more like his father than his mother, though his mother is surely inside him as well. He learned how to work hard by observing her as well as him.

His parents' migration to Australia dislodged him painfully from London, but the new land in which he found himself more than made up for what he had lost. Had he stayed in London he might have become that man in the flat above a shop in Seven Kings or Rainham, but he might well have simply been trapped by pinched possibilities and lived in the creases of time. Worse, the shadows of those two schools might have covered him completely. Australia was light as well as heat. Yet his parents' journey out of Essex unsettled him at some great depth, its tremors never really ended, and the bush was right that day when it said to him that he didn't belong there. He could see the landscape around him but could not feel the one hidden beneath it, the one that would make it home. In the end, after much internal debate, he migrated himself. He affirmed his parents' act, but in an unexpected way, by moving to the United States. Home for him lay in the future, not in the past; it was always somewhere he had to find. The man he became was caught in a narrative larger than his own, and one day he realized that he had unraveled the family secrets even before he knew them: he had become Catholic—another migration—and had married a Jew. The religion took; the marriage didn't. But when he regained his balance after the turmoil of divorce and annulment, once again he found himself dating a Jewish girl for a while. We write the pronoun "I" so easily, yet as life lengthens it sometimes seems that someone else, leaning over one's shoulder, is writing it for us. When we spin around, quickly, no one is there.

———— ▼ ————

A little checking of public records when I was living in America many years later showed that Nan had been born with the surname Ball. There was no change by Deed Poll. Did Mum know that? If she did, why did she say what she did? Was something else being hidden by Granddad, Nan, or her? I will never know. Further checking traced the matrilineal line back a few generations, and then it wavered and vanished: I found out enough to see that the surname Ball was a common one among Polish Jews. I became interested, for the only time in my life, with tracing the ancestry of my parents—but after a day or two I stopped sitting before the computer for hour on hour. I had found the birth certificate of my sister, born two years before my parents married, and then, a minute later, I found the birth certificate of my mother, who was born three months after my grandparents were married. Then I tried to go back further, found a long list of uncles and aunts, but was never sure if I had stumbled and lost my way; there were so few names ever said out loud when I was a child, and the photographs in the album almost never had names attached to them. Try as I might, no lead came my way to tell me anything about my father's father. He's lost in a thick London fog of over a century ago, and perhaps that is exactly what he wanted.

I came to the brink of getting a professional to do the work of tracing the family lines, but never returned the message left on my cell phone. After all, I had already lived decades of a life whose vanishing points had been determined through stories over drinks in the East End, and I did not want yet another division of myself if those stories were proven to be without base. What difference would it have made to me? I was Catholic in my religion, not Jewish, and I had chosen it of my own free will. And yet the question pierced me nonetheless. I kept the message on my cell phone; it is still there, and some days I wonder if I will return it. The woman's voice is clear, clean, American, and I know that, for a substantial fee, she is inviting me to hear other voices, fainter, with other accents, from Norfolk and Wales, but I fear that they will tell me less than I want to know. I would like to hear those Polish voices. I would like to know what they made of their new lives in Brick Lane and thereabouts. Yet I fear that no expensive charting of the Ball family will let me hear a word from them, even if it gives me some names and some dates. They would have been too poor to be remembered by anyone other than people like themselves.

But the body remembers; it knows everything, every secret that is passed on from generation to generation, and unlike those grandfathers and grandmothers, those fathers and mothers, those uncles and aunts, it will freely tell us what it knows when asked properly. So, when my elder daughter, Sarah, gave me a DNA kit as a Christmas present last year, I knew that my body would tell me the truth whenever I asked it to do so. One day several months later I was ready to open the kit. I found a test tube there and instructions to spit into it. Quite a lot of spittle was needed, I discovered, and I spent a good fifteen minutes filling it up to the required line, almost retching at the end. But I produced enough, and I sent the tube on its way. Some weeks later, an email arrived with an analysis: about fifty-five percent of my background was British and Irish, French and German forebears comprised about twenty-four percent, with seventeen and a half percent of other family members coming from Northwestern Europe, and two-and-a-bit percent coming from Scandinavia. Less than a tenth of a percent was Ashkenazi Jewish, coming into my genealogy in the seventeenth century. The banjo story about the matrilineal line being Jewish and going back to Poland was groundless. My maternal haplogroup appears to have come from western Siberia, and my paternal haplogroup from Northern Europe. Those Jewish Poles who have lived with me, inside me, for forty years seem to have been characters in a narrative, not people who lived in Poland and then London; and I feel as though I have lived most of my life in a story that never happened.

— ▾ —

Most days of the week I walk to my office at the University of Virginia along the West Range, and sometimes I stop at No. 13, which was Edgar Allen Poe's room when he was an undergraduate here from February to December of 1826, and which the Raven Society faithfully maintains. I've stood with many friends and visitors as they peer through the glass door at the hard chairs, small bed, and the desk with a raven perched on it. Usually, they'll quote a line or two from "The Raven," sometimes only a word: "Nevermore." In recent years, it's no longer the artifacts in the room that draw my attention, and Poe's poetry has never gripped me, but lines come to mind from stories such as "The Gold Bug," "The Purloined Letter," and "The Man in the Crowd." In that last story we're told, right at the start, "There are some secrets which do not permit themselves to be told." The narrator goes on to evoke men on their deathbeds who refuse to reveal things they have done. Poe himself claimed to be able to break any cipher at all, and he hid messages in some of his writings. But a message must be encrypted in order to be broken.

As I think back over my childhood, I wonder if there were things I missed—remarks, glances, sighs, silences, whispers—that floated on the surface of family life that, if seen or heard properly, would have revealed what my parents kept hidden from me and perhaps even from themselves. Maybe there were, or maybe it is all too easy now to find those things in memory, for memory will adjust itself to fit our sense of the past when that sense begins to take on a literary form. Poe thought those secrets that cannot be told are linked to the essence of crime, but I think that there are also innocent secrets. I cannot even begin to chart my secret life as a boy in London, that life in which the outside world seemed insubstantial and vaguely unreal. Of course, that boy also knew the world was perfectly real; it pushed up against him, hard at times, which only made him withdraw again and sometimes a little more deeply into a dark land only he knew and trusted. I know that from time to time he saw that world as it was, felt it intensely, and remembered it closely, as if it were a dangerous animal he must never forget was following him day and night. Even when he was at Eastbrookland it was there, waiting next to his bicycle when he started to turn homewards. Through the act of remembering those moments, he formed his own album of memories, one that no one else could ever open. It has been kept closed, for the most part, for fifty years. Within it are other images, too, which betray hints of things wholly internal, fears, to be sure, yet also stubbornness: a resilience built of retreat.

So much of that secret life cannot be told; it dissipates as I look at it, parts easily, as though it were nothing, is entirely passive. I look to feel, once more, something of his loneliness and bewilderment at home and in the classroom, but can make out less than I know was there. As I have been writing these pages, I have probed him to know the exact quality, the precise degree of fierceness, of this emotion or that one, but each time he turns away and will not let me near him. I have come to wonder if the boy I was somehow knew that the greatest power he had was his passivity in the face of his family and the schools he attended, and I have tried to weigh how much of that passivity was owing to detachment and how much to insensibility. Certainly it was a strong seal, one that kept his London years inviolate, and it might be his own subtle way of retaining his hidden life, of keeping it even from the man he would become. Looking at him now, after two months of writing by day and by night, I see that we are in stalemate. I have told his story, as though from the outside, and he has not let me tell the story of his inner life and his abiding silences, except for when they have slipped out by accident.

——▼——

"School": at times the word still runs icy fingers up my spine and makes my stomach rise. Or I wake up, even now, at a nightmare: I am still in Fergie's class, trying to do some problem that I can't make head or tail of. Now that I am a professor and an American, well used to American idioms, I still sometimes feel ashamed for a moment or two when I hear the University of Virginia called a "school," as though I belong to and represent something I loathe. I am instantly taken back fifty years, as though life were an immense game of snakes and ladders and every so often I land right on that big snake's head on the top few squares and slide all the way back to the start. I do not curse my years at Thomas Arnold and Eastbrook; I simply feel sick at the very memory of them, and I have written these words in order to be rid of that feeling, if possible. "School" still means a looming grayness that threatened to engulf me forever. If I have become a teacher, it is partly because I did not want other people to have that sense of bafflement and loneliness and partly because it was the best way to erase all that "school" meant to me as a child.

Most of my early childhood has been thoroughly erased in any case. Almost all the family I have evoked has passed away. Cousin Albert survived until his early sixties, outliving almost all of those who bent so intently over tea and buns to discuss his fate, although his rare Asian disease was never properly diagnosed. Some years ago my sister, only in her early seventies, was found to have incipient dementia and had to be taken into care in a retirement village in Durack, right next to Inala. And it was there she died. The schools in London remain, brighter and happier places when I have visited them in recent years; even so, I shuddered as I walked their corridors, just as I shake when I wake at night after nightmares of still being there. Corinda Primary School was moved from the corner of Clivedon Avenue and Oxley Road, but not very far at all: it was relocated further down the Avenue. The old premises were first used as a School Support Center, and then, several years later, were turned into high-density housing. Oxley State High School was decommissioned in 2000; it's now a ghostly, abandoned place, entirely overgrown by the bush that was cut down so severely when it was built. The Baptist preacher, Raymond Schalchlin, died of a heart attack in his fifties when fighting a fire in Arkansas; his son, my friend Philip, served time for rape and died a decade ago. Beckton Gas Works was closed down in 1969, when I was in year nine at Oxley High; my father was right to think about moving when he did. For a while, all that remained was a heap of toxic waste. Nowadays there is almost nothing left on the site, only a little rubbish that can be glimpsed if you look quickly at the right moment when driving down the A1020. Eastbrookend was cleaned up in the early 1990s, trees were planted, grass was sown, and all the broken houses from the Blitz removed; it

opened as Eastbrookend Country Park in 1995, and now people go fishing there. It is almost impossible to locate the places
Eddie, Kevin, and I visited and invested with so much meaning,
and I will never find the lake with the swans.

————— ▼ —————

Writing these pages, day after day, I wake up in the early hours,
as I haven't done in many years. And when I do I ask myself:
What have I lost? The boy I was in London lost a milky insulation against the world, where he could withdraw for days and
weeks on end, where he communed mostly with himself, and
from where he looked out, fitfully, and on his own terms, onto
a world to which he was convinced he didn't belong. That it was
scary, I do not doubt, but try as I might, I cannot fully recover
what it meant to be that way, or what it meant to him to be so
deep inside himself. It is something I greatly want to know but
cannot. No traction is to be found there.

When my thoughts get that far and sleep is still a long way
off, I ask myself: What do I fear? It is a more difficult question,
because I fear that I might one day begin to understand again
what that boy knew so well, that I might find it comforting, that
I might lose my hold on the world I have made, in reading book
after book, in teaching, in writing, in having children and friends,
and simply conducting a life as best I can. I fear to lose the clarity of mind that I have gained. That the window might spring
shut again seems unlikely after all these years, but I know people, not much older than I am, who have begun to suffer from
one or another form of dementia. If I don't have an absolute
fear of dementia, as some of my friends do, perhaps it is only
because I started life living in a mental fog. I tell myself that I
would merely be returning home, back to a thicker version of
what Qohelet calls *hebel*, a mist or vapor that gets translated as
"emptiness," even "vanity." Perhaps, in the end, I will be sur-

prised: the home I have long figured to be ahead of me will be so but at the same time will also be in my deepest past. Certainly I fear to lose the contact I have with that boy, who steps away each week of my life, especially now that I have been on his trail, and who, after all, is the one to whom I owe everything. The more I look for him, the more surely he retreats. I saw him plain only after it was too late, when he had allowed the warmth of Brisbane to lure him out a little way, and when he was hurt by words he heard when almost awake. Sometimes when I look suddenly at him, I see a cicada shell.

And then, before I can sleep again, I ask myself: What do I want? It is the hardest question of all. I tell myself I want nothing of my childhood. Then I say, with equal passion, that I want it all back again. And I say that I want to understand that boy I was. None of it hangs together. I get up before it is light these past two months, after restless nights, and write more in the hope that I can hold myself close to the boy I was or at least begin to understand him and so more of the man he became.

—— ▼ ——

Childhood ends, and then it ends again, and then it ends yet again. For me, it ended in that algebra class. What happened that afternoon? I thought about it for years, trying to recreate the moments before and after, and trying to register each change I felt. I could never write about it in a poem, although I have told people about it, especially those who have been worried about one or another of their children not doing so well at school or seeming to be lost deep in themselves. I know what it is to be regarded as a slow child, even a hopeless case, but far worse is the experience of being loved on condition of fitting into the institutions of the world. The brutality of my schooling in London was hard, but many people have had far worse, and one can grow around and beyond such things; it is more of a challenge

to overcome the effects of silences and gaps, one's own withdrawal from affection in which one cannot believe. I have come
to understand that sudden wrenching in the algebra class as God
releasing me after years of insulation against the world. I had
been sequestered, living in a fog that hid me from pain as well
as from pleasure, and that afternoon was the right and proper
time for all that to change. It was not a passage from Dark-Land,
as I thought from time to time in the decade or so that followed,
for that Land is a strong one, capable of more subtle movements
than those who walk through it, and the hill one tries to climb in
order to get away from it has many twisting paths that lead back
to its start.

My childhood ended in another way with the deaths of my
grandparents, which left only one wall between death and me.
With the deaths of my parents, no wall was left. You can feel the
chill air of freedom, and perhaps it is only then that you also feel
the finer edge of the word "life." Yet the end is not complete,
even then. We are always children when we are asleep, and my
childhood sometimes possesses me in the night, more power-
fully than when I was a boy. I wake up in darkness to find that I
am not in that classroom at Thomas Arnold or Eastbrook after
all, not cycling home through the dark wet streets of the East
End, and must calm myself by reciting the "Our Father" or some
lines of poetry, by recounting to myself a difficult concept in philosophy, and then I can return to sleep. Finally, for me at least,
childhood never truly ends; it continues, beneath the patina of
life, in the interpretation of those silences and gaps, the meditation on secrets kept for decades, never knowing for sure if one
has read them correctly or if far more work of some undisclosed
kind is required, work arising from moments hidden in time that
might spring to life again by virtue of one accidental association
or another and that might explain more: this hard word, that
desolate look. When something is withheld from intelligence,

from ingenuity, from the finalities of accepted grief and regret, and even from ordinary human sorrow, when it is a matter of understanding things never said, or said far too late, gestures never made, or made only after death, one can never know if one is moving ahead, to the side, or back.

Glossary

ACER: Australian Council for Educational Research

APPLE CHARLOTTE: Australian delicacy: Baked apples in a small cake with thick cream on top.

BABYCHAM: A sparkling drink, made from fermented pears, popular especially among young women in Britain in the 1960s and 1970s for whom it had the aura of sophistication.

BANJO: London expression for a dead-end road that ends in a circle.

BARNARDO'S HOMES: Thomas John Barnado established a charity to care for vulnerable children, especially orphans. Several orphanages were built in London.

BEBERT: The name of Louis-Ferdinand Céline's beloved cat, and one of the most famous cats of French literature. He appears in several of Céline's novels, including *Féerie pour un autre fois* (1954) and *Normance* (1954).

BORSTAL: Special schools in Britain, run by HM Prison Service, established to reform delinquent children. The expression "Borstal school" comes from India.

BREAD PUDDING: A dessert popular in the East End of London, as well as in many other places. It is made from dry bread, eggs, milk, sugar, cinnamon, and dried fruit.

BRYLCREEM: Men's hair styling product, which keeps hair slicked back very firmly.

BUNDLE: East End slang for a fight.

CATAPULT: A slingshot, usually made from a Y cut of a tree's new growth, with elastic and a leather square for holding a stone, marble, or staple. More sophisticated ones were made of metal, and were hard to come by.

CHEESECAKE: The English cheesecake is made of layers of pastry, jam, icing and coconut; it is not to be confused with American cheesecake.

CHIKO ROLL: Australian version of spring rolls, larger and chewier.

CHOOK: Australian colloquialism for a chicken.

CONKER: A chestnut with a hole bored through it, which is suspended from a string with a knot at the end. Playing conkers involves one person holding a conker while the other person takes a swipe at it with his. Whoever's conker breaks is the loser.

CWA: Country Women's Association

DALEKS: Alien race of mutants, committed to universal domination, in *Doctor Who*.

DDT: Dichlorodiphenyltrichloroethane was used to kill insects, especially mosquitoes, in Brisbane. An odor became apparent only when large quantities of it were used.

DLP: Democratic Labour Party: a right-wing political party very active in the 1960s in Australia. Its leader from 1965 to 1973 was Vince Gair.

DOCTOR DOLITTLE:	Dr. John Dolittle is the main character in twelve novels written by Hugh Lofting, beginning with *The Story of Doctor Dolittle: Being the History of his Peculiar Life at Home and Astonishing Adventures in Foreign Parts* (1920) and ending with *Doctor Dolittle's Puddleby Adventures* (1952).
ESSO BLUE:	A sort of paraffin sold by "The Paraffin Man" who came door to door in the East End in the 1960s.
EKKA:	Brisbanites use the word affectionately to denote the Royal Queensland Show, held each year in August in the Brisbane Showgrounds.
ELEVEN-PLUS:	From its inception in 1944, the Eleven-Plus examination was taken in the last year of primary school in Britain; it determined which sort of high school one could attend: Grammar School or a Comprehensive School. Considerable criticism of the examination has been made on the ground that it was biased against working-class children, and it ended in 2008.
FAGGOTS:	English expression: a rissole made of cheap cuts of food, usually pig's heart, liver, and belly, mixed with breadcrumbs.
GUY:	In Britain an effigy of Guy Fawkes (1570-1606) is burned each November 5. Fawkes, a Catholic, was a member of the Gunpowder Plot, which sought to kill the Protestant King James I. The plot failed and he was executed for treason. (His sentence was to be hung, drawn and quartered, but his neck broke in the first stage and so was not alive for the grisly second and third parts of the execution.) November 5 is deemed a day to celebrate the King's deliverance, and children with a guy are given small change by passersby as a reward for making it.

HODGE:	One of Samuel Johnson's cats, made famous by James Boswell in his depiction of the cat in his *Life of Samuel Johnson, LLD* (1791).
JACK DASH:	English Communist, Trade Unionist, and deep supporter of the London dock workers.
JAKIES:	Men who drank methylated spirits and frequented the Beckton Marshes.
JAMBOREE BAG:	A small paper bag, sometimes called a Lucky Bag, sold to children in London in the 1960s. Each bag contained cheap candy and a novelty item, such as a plastic whistle or temporary tattoo.
JEOFFRY:	Christopher Smart's cat as celebrated in his *Jubilate Agno* (1759-63)
KNOCK DOWN GINGER:	English expression: children ring a doorbell, and then run and hide; the procedure is repeated until the man or woman opening the door is completely exasperated.
KRAY BROTHERS:	Ronnie and Reggie Kray were two of the most successful gangsters in London in the 1950's and 60's.
LUCKY BAG:	See "JAMBOREE BAG."
MARGE:	English and Australian abbreviation for margarine.
MARY QUANT:	British fashion designer, popular in Mod designs in the 1960s.
MICK:	English expression: To take the mick out of someone is to poke fun at him or her.
MILK BAR:	Australian expression: a small shop that sells fast food, candy, newspapers, magazines, milk, and other small goods.
MOSQUITO COIL:	Australian expression: mosquito-repelling incense, shaped into a spiral and slow burning.
MOZZIE:	Australian colloquialism for mosquito.
NEVER NEVER:	English expression for "Buy Now, Pay Later."

NHS: National Health Service.

NISSEN HUT: Prefabricated steel structures made from a half-cylinder of corrugated iron. Built for military use and, later, as family housing.

OODLE   Language spoken by Bill and Ben the Flowerpot
PODDLE: Men on their TV Show in England in the 1960s.

PANGUR BAN: The cat of an unknown eighth or ninth century monk who wrote a poem comparing the two of them.

PEASHOOTER: English expression: a blowpipe in which one blows dried peas (or anything similar) hard at someone.

PLIMSOLL: English expression for light canvas shoe.

PEASE   A thick pudding made from split yellow peas, and
PUDDING: often served in England with bacon or a ham hock.

PETER PAN: A statue of Peter Pan is in Kensington Gardens, near Hyde Park; it was commissioned by J. M. Barrie and built by Sir George Frampton who erected in 1912.

PIMM'S CUP: Pimm's and ginger ale, garnished with fruit and cucumber.

POLLY   Australian candy: a waffle tube filled with marsh-
WAFFLE: mallow and covered with chocolate.

POM: Australian colloquialism for a British immigrant.

PORT: Queensland expression for a backpack worn by schoolchildren.

POSTIE: Australian colloquialism for postman. In Brisbane in the 1960s, posties delivered mail twice a day and once on Saturdays on bikes, blowing a whistle at each delivery.

POT: Queensland expression for a small glass of beer; a larger class is a schooner.

QUEENS-LANDER:	Queensland expression: a house on stilts with corrugated iron and a wide verandah; common in Brisbane and elsewhere in Queensland.
RABBIT PUNCH:	English expression: a chop with the side of one's hand to the back of someone's neck.
ROCK:	English expression: a stick of hard boiled sugar candy, usually peppermint or spearmint flavored, sold at seaside resorts in England, and usually with the name of the resort printed in the white candy going all the way down.
RUNNING UP:	English and Australian expression: sewing a dress.
SAUSAGE ROLLS:	English and Australian fast food: sausage mince and onions baked in puff pastry, served with ketchup.
SAVALOY:	A bright red, highly seasoned sausage, which is usually boiled; often served in England with Pease Pudding.
SHOW BAG:	A bag containing samples of chocolates and other delicacies that are sold at booths at the Ekka (the Brisbane Exhibition, or Show).
SINGER:	A sort of sewing machine.
SNOWBALL:	A drink composed of advocaat and lemonade in more or less equal parts.
SPAM:	Precooked spiced ham in a can; it was widely eaten in working-class Britain during World War II and after.
SPOTTED DICK:	British desert: a cylindrical suet pudding, made with dried fruit, steamed in a tea towel, and served with hot custard.
SUNSHINE:	A form of address in the East End, sometimes positive but mostly sarcastic and, in the instance when I use it in this memoir, threatening.

TARDIS:	The police telephone box in *Doctor Who* that became the fixed form of the Doctor's time traveling machine.
TATTOO:	Military musical performance with a display of precision marching.
TIZER:	Red colored soft drink available in Britain.
TRANSFER:	A temporary tattoo.
WALL'S	An English ice cream company that has been going strong since the late eighteenth century. In the 1960s blue, yellow, and white ice cream vans went from street to street playing "Greensleeves," which alerted children (and many adults) to the presence of the van.
WALLY:	London expression for a pickled cucumber, usually served with fish and chips.
WILLIES:	English expression for the creeps.
WINKLE-PICKERS:	Shoe worn by young men in London in the 1950s and 1960s, as a sign of their love for rock n' roll.
XXXX	Sign for "4X Beer," a Queenslander's beer of choice.

Photo credit: Sashanna Hart

KEVIN HART is the author of eleven poetry collections including *Wild Track: New and Selected Poems* and *Barefoot*. His most recent books are *Lands of Likeness: For a Poetics of Contemplation*, which represents his Gifford Lectures for 2019-2023, and *Contemplation: The Movements of the Soul*. He is the Jo Rae Wright University Professor in the School of Divinity, at Duke University, and lives with his wife and son in Durham, NC.